History of the Cossacks

William Cresson

Published 2017 by Didactic Press

All rights reserved.

CONTENTS

THE ORIGIN OF THE "FREE PEOPLE" 7

THE ZAPOROGIAN COSSACKS 22

YERMAK AND THE COSSACK CONQUEST OF SIBERIA 39

BOGDAN HMELNICKY; A COSSACK NATIONAL HERO ... 54

THE STRUGGLE FOR THE UKRAINE 75

MAZEPPA 83

THE END OF THE FREE UKRAINE: LITTLE RUSSIA 99

POUGATCHEV 111

THE HETMAN PLATOV 129

THE COSSACKS OF TO-DAY: ORGANIZATION AND GOVERNMENT 148

THE COSSACKS OF TO-DAY: THE DON 158

THE FRONTIERS OF EUROPE 168

THE ORIGIN OF THE "FREE PEOPLE"

THE level plains and steppes of South Russia were known to the ancients as the broad channel followed by the ebb and flow of every fresh wave of conquest or migration passing between Europe and Asia. The legions of Rome and Byzance found this territory as impossible to occupy by military force as the high seas. The little known history of "Scythia" – from the earliest times until the thirteenth century of the Christian era – presents a confused picture of barbarous tribes pressing one upon another, the stronger driving the weaker before them from the more favoured hunting grounds. Often, voluntarily or by force, the victors included the vanquished in their own "superior" civilization. There are many reasons why it is difficult or impossible to follow with any degree of certainty the national history of these races. "Their long-forgotten quarrels, their interminglings and separations, above all the constant changes in their names and habitat make the study of their history as difficult as it is unprofitable." (Lesur, *Histoire des Kosaques*.)

This ignorance of the changes – political and economical – which are constantly taking place along the amorphous racial frontiers of Eastern Europe, has continued to our own times. But at recurrent intervals these Slav borderlands separating the Occident from the Orient become the scene of political upheavals so vast in their consequences that the very foundations of European civilization are shaken in their turn.

The great Tartar invasion which, during the thirteenth century, swept out of Asia and spread across the steppes of Southern Russia, was an occurrence of such magnitude that its echoes travelled to the most distant states of Europe. The arrival of fugitive bands of Khomans, Black Bulgars, and other wild steppe tribesmen at the court of Bela IV, King of Hungary, first spread the fame and terror of these new invaders. From these refugees and their descriptions of the enemy the sovereigns of Christendom learned with horror of the fate which in the short space of a few months had overtaken the most powerful strongholds of the princes of Rus and Muscovy. Even the Poles – whose more civilized and warlike state was generally considered the bulwark separating the "barbarians" of ancient Scythia from the communities of Europe – had been forced to make the best terms possible: by paying a degrading tribute to the invaders. The powers of Europe now beheld upon the frontiers of their own empires an enemy far more redoubtable than the Saracen "infidels" against whom they had waged their mystical crusades. Turning from his dream of rescuing the Holy Sepulchre the Emperor Frederick II exercised all his eloquence to unite the Christian princes in a league against the Mongols. The Roman Pontiff, fearing for the Christian religion, preached a Holy War. Saint Louis prepared to march in person against the barbarians.

HISTORY OF THE COSSACKS

"All of civilized Europe was given over to anxiety and apprehension. The Tartars were represented, as monsters living upon human flesh." "Even the most reasonable believed that the end of the world was at hand. The people of Gog and Magog advancing under the command of the Antichrist were about to bring about the destruction of the universe." Suddenly, as though by common agreement or following some general command, the widely scattered hordes of horsemen turned once more towards the East, finally settling in great armed camps upon the fertile steppes near the shores of the Volga. In this inexplicable action, as mysterious as their first appearance from the heart of Asia, the writers of the time perceived the hand of an unseen Providence. The avenging wrath of the Deity had been turned aside by the intercession of the priests and holy men of Christendom. Yet complete as the conquest of the Tartars appeared to be it was not destined to outlast the century which saw its rise. As usual in Oriental despotisms the seeds of its dissolution came from within.

The first result of these disaffections – notably a revolt of the Nogai tribesmen against the princes of the Golden Horde – was the disappearance of the crude administrative system exercised by the Tartar rulers over the old tribes of the steppes. These began once more to reassert their independence. Bands of Scythian refugees, Khosars, Khomans and "Khosaks," began to leave the marshy deltas of the great rivers such as the Don and Dnieper – where they had found in common a precarious refuge – and mounted on horses stolen from the Tartars returned to their familiar haunts. Here a terrible desolation spoke everywhere of "Tartar Peace." How complete had been the destruction of whole tribes and settlements of the previous inhabitants – caught by the overwhelming avalanche of Tartar horsemen – is Pictured by the monkish chroniclers of a previous generation. In Hakluyt's *Voyages* these travellers describe how "for over three hundred leagues" they passed through great fields of whitening bones, "the only signs that might recall the presence of previous inhabitants of the steppes."

The wars of the princes of Tartary with the revolted Nogai and the struggles of the latter with the Russians now gave to the miserable remnants of the ancient lords of Scythia an opportunity to recover something of their ascendency, over the wildest and most deserted parts of the steppes. As these scattered tribesmen became more skilled in desert warfare; both Russians and Tartars occasionally sought their alliance and the aid of their ill-armed cavalry in settling their quarrels. But whether gathered in armed camps or *Slovods*, or else leading an errant nomad life, these "war bands," composed of refugees and renegades of every origin, were a constant menace to the frontiers of their more civilized neighbours; pirating on the great rivers and attacking the caravans of Russian or Tartar merchants with indifferent zeal. In the precarious existence of these rovers, we find the first traces of the frontier "civilization" of the Cossacks.

No problem of Russian history has given rise to more controversy than that of the origin of the Cossack race. It now appears established that the influence of the geographic and climatic conditions which exist on the steppes, modifying to a common type the characteristics of the peoples and tribes (often of wholly different origin) who in turn have inhabited the ancient lands of the Seyths — is the paramount factor in solving this problem. The tracing of blood ties and relationships would therefore seem of less importance than an understanding of the conditions under which the characteristic Cossack civilization has been developed.

The Russian word *Kasak* — of which "Cossack" is the English equivalent — still signifies in several Tartar dialects a "Horseman" or

"Rover." By a not unnatural association of ideas this term has been adopted at different times and in widely separated localities as a tribal name by nomad peoples of the steppes. But the attempt not infrequently made to trace a direct connection between these tribes and the famous *Kasaki* of modern Russia is generally based upon far-fetched historical analogies.

In Clarke's famous "Travels in the Ukraine" the ingenious theory is advanced that the country of "Kasachia" mentioned by Constantine Porphyrogenetes was the original homeland of the modern "tribes" of Russia which have taken the general name of Kasak or Cossack. But the relative unimportance of this people lost among powerful neighbours whose history has survived to the present day is the strongest argument against such a supposition. Moreover, as we have already pointed out, other tribes of this name have more than once risen to temporary importance in the annals of the steppes.

It was not until the latter half of the fifteenth century that the ebbing tide of Tartar invasion, which for nearly two centuries had submerged the richest lands of the great Russian plain, once more opened to settlement from the North the rich steppes of the "Black Earth" district, and the scarcely less fertile lands to the South and East. During this long period of subjection the Russian nation had been held back from its richest heritage.

Scattered among the Finnish aborigines of the great northern forests – in that fabulous land of "Cimmerian darkness" where, as Herodotus states, the inhabitants "spend half their time in slumber" – the men of "Rus" had kept alive the faith of their ancestors while learning their long lesson of patience and endurance. Thus it came about that so many of the old centres and cities of Holy Russia are found today in the most barren and unattractive parts of the great Russian plain.

When the prairies of the Ukraine – the "border land" – had ceased to be the hunting grounds of roving nomads, and the Asiatic hordes had withdrawn with their flocks and herds to the oases of their native deserts, the peasant population of Northern Russia became filled with a restless fever for emigration. Out of the dark fir wilderness came bands of pioneers, – dazzled by the bright sunlight of the steppes, – pressing ever southward. Thus settlers of true Russian blood began once more to populate the war-worn plains of Scythia where free land and, dearer still, personal freedom rewarded the daring of the adventurer.

While fear and hunger had kept them submissively huddled about the wooden fortresses of the *boyars*, no laws had been necessary to chain the peasants to the glebe. Serfdom now began in Russia at the time when the feudal system of Europe was sinking into decay. For when the princes and nobles of these northern principalities found their *apanages* and broad grants of forest land fast reverting to wilderness through the flight of the agricultural laborers, legal steps were taken to preserve their "rights." In edicts of Ivan the Terrible and Boris Godounov, we find the legislative traces of this great southern movement. Yet, in spite of terrible punishments and laws enacted to keep the peasants from roving, the *moujiki* continued to join themselves to the remnants of the wild Asiatic tribes and the no less barbarous "Cossacks" of their own race, who had established themselves in vagabond communities following close upon the receding frontier of Tartar invasion.

It would appear that about this time the term Cossack or *Kasak* was first used to describe a "masterless man," one who refused to identify himself with the *Krestianin* or ordinary agricultural laborer (a class about to fall wholly into the condition of serfdom). The same word may previously have been used by the Tartars after their conquest of Russia to denote tribesmen who, refusing to settle in towns or colonies, preferred to continue the nomad and adventurous life of their ancestors. The name also began to be applied to soldier-mercenaries from the steppe "war bands," who, while maintaining the warlike traditions of this wandering life, refused to become incorporated among the men-at-arms attached to the great *boyars* or to take permanent service in the paid militia formed by the Tsars after the reign of Ivan IV.

To the brutal methods of Tartar dominion may be ascribed traits which have left a deep mark on the government and policy of the empire of the Tsars. Russian historians are now the first to recognize the depth and force of this influence. Naturally democratic in their ideals and personal relations, long subjection to the Tartars taught the Slav people subservience, and (together with later principles borrowed by Peter the Great from the Prussian system) furnished their rulers a model of greedy despotism and autocratic power. Even the excesses of revolution in our own day show the persistence in the Russian state of these pernicious alien influences.

Under the ruthless sword-strokes of Czar Vasili, and his successor Ivan the Terrible, began the up. building of the great modern state of Russia — engulfing in an ever-widening circle of dominion the liberties of lesser princelings and the *bourgeoisie* of the forest "City Republics." Such was the fate of Pskov, of the Free Republic of Vologda and the city of "LordNovgorod the Great."

Meanwhile, on the vast southern plains, under the leadership of dispossessed *boyars*, renegade Polish nobles, Turkish janissaries, or even some far-wandering French or German adventurer, the characteristic civilization of the Ukraine Cossack communities steadily grew and strengthened. Recruited from sturdy vagabonds of every race and clan, "stolen youths, thieves and patriots" armed with the weapons they had brought with them from Russia or with the bows and arrows of their Tartar neighbours, they fought for and gradually obtained the right to exist and to remain free.

In view of the importance of geographical conditions upon the inhabitants of these plains, it now becomes necessary to consider at greater length some of the phenomena peculiar to the South Russian Steppes. For thousands of years – until the coming of the railways in recent times – the problems of life on the Russian prairies must have presented themselves again and again under the same inevitable forms. The nations who established their permanent home in this fertile "smiling wilderness" were all endowed with similar characteristics. Their lives were passed on horseback and their existence depended on their skill as breeders of half-wild cattle and hunters of wary game. The Greek legend of the Centaurs was, in their case, scarcely an exaggeration. In plains so vast as to be almost without natural limits or defensible frontiers a necessary factor of effective occupation became the ability to defend a chosen area at any moment in hand to hand encounters with a mobile foe. Highways of trade and communication could be shifted – in the absence of all natural obstacles – with the same ease that a new course can be steered at sea. For this reason, the objects of steppe warfare were different from those of ordinary strategy. In reading of the military campaigns of the Ukraine we must often be prepared to draw our comparisons from naval rather than from land operations.

The country known as the Ukraine, where the characteristic Cossack civilization arose and developed, is, as the name indicates, a continental "border land," neither European nor Asiatic. On the wide steppes of the Black Sea basin even the climatic influences of north and south meet without blending. Thus, while during the short summer months a true southern climate prevails, yet the return of winter is marked by a cold nearly subarctic in its intensity.

In the famous Black Earth region about Kiev and Poltava, the brief harvest season forms the climax of a miracle of growth. Under the rays of an almost tropical sun the wide fields of grain change from silvery green to tawny gold in the space of days rather than weeks. But with the advent of another season the arctic winds sweep straight from the Polar seas, unchecked by hill or mountain range, all conquering, across the whole level expanse of New Russia. Upon the sunny steppes tightens once more the icy grip of the Empire of the North. There can be no softening of the fibre, no slackening of the powers of sturdy resistance which above all else characterize the Russian race in the population of such a land. Both in physique and temperament the lithe dark inhabitant of the Ukraine presents the type of a southerner. While sprung from the same stock he is as distinct from the blond dweller of the north as the Provençal of France is different from the blue-eyed Norman. To his Slav nature the brief vision of southern summer has added a touch of imagination, a capacity for boisterous enjoyment, lacking, at any rate less apparent, in the Russian of "Muscovy."

Before the coming of the farmer and his plough the plains of the Ukraine were everywhere covered by high waving grasses, similar to the vanished prairies of far western America, or the *vegas* of southern Andalusia. Often this growth is so thick that a horseman can only with difficulty force his way, and the half-wild cattle almost disappear in the richness of their pasture. Not even a tree or bush breaks the straight sky line of the horizon. Meandering in wide curves, often with a scarcely perceptible fall from north to south, four great rivers form the most striking geographical features of these plains: the Dnieper, the Don, and farther eastward the mighty

"Mother Volga" and her lesser companion, the Ural. "Her rivers," says Rambaud, "are the only allies of man against Russia's great enemy — distance." In winter their frozen surface, and in summer their broad tide, are the principal pathways from one part of this great land to another.

It was upon the shores of the great river Dnieper, known to the Ancients as the Borysthenes, that the first permanent Cossack communities established had their settlements.

*

By slow degrees, under the increasing influence of peasant immigration from the North (bringing with it the religion of Russia and such rude civilization as the northern woods had developed) the Asiatic and "tribal" features of Cossack life began to disappear. During the early days of the XVIth century they had so strengthened their hold upon the broad lands lying between the Dnieper and the Don, that we find the terms "Free Cossacks of the Ukraine" and even "The Republic of the Don" used to describe their settlements. But the early condition of these wandering Cossack communities must have been a matter of scorn even to the primitive tribes of the Boujiak Tartars who were their neighbours. Family life or social organization were all but impossible under the conditions of their harried existence. Some of these steppe bands (as we shall later observe in the case of the "Brotherhood" of the Zaporogian Cossacks, inhabiting the shores and islands of the Dnieper) even appear to have forbidden the presence of women in their camps.

In the growing Cossack settlements or slovods only the sturdiest of the children were allowed to survive. As a preparation for a lifelong struggle with the forces of the steppes "their mothers were wont to plunge them at birth either into a snowdrift or in a mixture of salt and water." None of the scanty provisions of the tribe could be wasted upon weaklings or those of unpromising physique. When scarcely able to walk, the young Cossacks were placed on horseback and "soon learned to swim wide rivers thus mounted" (ibid). At an early age they were only allowed food when by their unaided skill with bow and arrow they had brought down the wild game which supplied the family cook-pot. The clothing of the first Cossack tribesmen was contrived from sheepskins or the hides of wild beasts. Only the chieftains of the highest rank were able to afford garments of coarsely woven cloth dyed in brilliant colours (ibid). In case of sickness the Cossack remedy was to mount on horseback and, after galloping across the plain until both steed and rider were exhausted, to open a small vein in the shoulder of their mount and drink the warm blood.

As their flocks and herds multiplied upon the generous pasturage there grew up in the former "Tartar desert" a characteristic light-hearted civilization peculiar to the steppes. In the Little Russians of the present day we may still trace the manners and customs of this Free Cossack ancestry. Moreover as their ability to resist the encroaching tyranny of the Russian boyars increased, the Free Cossacks sought an early opportunity to renew relations with their European kinsmen. A common danger and their mutual hatred of the Turks and Tartars were forces tending to unite them with their Christian kindred the Russians and Poles. But in Poland the feudal land holders could find no place in their aristocratic state for freemen not of the noble classes, while in Russia the condition of the *moujiki* warned the Cossacks against the dangers of a too binding alliance with the Tsar.

In order to secure the military aid of the Cossacks, the Polish kings were forced to allow them to establish lists or "Registers" of "Free Soldiers" to whom claim of serfage was relinquished by the feudal lords. These latter, however, always claimed possession of the lands occupied by the Cossacks and their right to liberty as a caste was never recognized. This, as we shall later see, was the cause of the great uprising ending in the separation of the Cossack Ukraine from the Polish crown.

In spite of these differences, however, the eastern Cossack steppes began, soon after the downfall of the Tartars, to be considered the defensive frontiers of both Poland and the Muscovite empire. The Cossack warriors of the Polish Ukraine, though clinging tenaciously to their liberties and denying any right on the part of an alien government to claim their services, often entered the feudal military companies of the Polish nobles as volunteers or paid men-at-arms, while farther to the eastward, their kindred entered the service of the Tsar.

The last stronghold of the Tartars in Russia – Kazan – was captured by Ivan the Terrible after a long siege ending October 2, 1551. We find in the list of troops taking part in these operations the presence noted of a large contingent of Cossacks: "Cossacks of the town and Cossacks of the country." These together with the newly-formed Russian streltzi or regular troops took a prominent part in the assault. From 1553 to 1555 Ivan completed his conquests along the whole course of the Volga, finally capturing Astrakhan near the shores of the Caspian. Their admiration for the Tsar's exploits against the common enemy, and perhaps a wholesome realization of the fact that his armies now controlled an easy base of approach to the strongholds of their "republic," led the Cossacks inhabiting the shores of the Don to place themselves under his protection. The Cossacks of the Dnieper remained, however, in the pay of Poland. Thus occurred the first great separation in the loose confederation of the "Free Companions of the Steppes."

After the more or less voluntary submission of the *"Free Cossacks of the*

Don" the Russian Tsars soon began to make use of their matchless skill in frontier warfare. An arrangement mutually favorable was now perfected and the Cossacks became the basis of a system of defensive militia policing the steppes against the Crimean Tartars. Although the Muscovite peasants were brave and (above all) docile foot soldiers, their usefulness as cavalry was limited. Previous to the time when Cossacks were enrolled for this purpose, it had been found necessary – in order to defend the open frontiers of Muscovy – to mobilize every year a force of about 65,000 men. Owing to the fact that the *rendezvous* chosen lay on the banks of the river Oka, this was called the annual "banks service." In the early days this duty had been performed by the feudal levies of the great *boyars*, whose serf and peasant troops attended the annual musters unwillingly and often at great inconvenience to themselves during the harvest season (a time therefore usually chosen by the Tartars for their raids). As early as 1571 a Russian *boyar*, Prince Borotinsky, began to employ a system of mixed Cossack and militia patrols which appears to have differed but little from the military colonies or *stanitzi* of the later Cossack "armies." During the seasons less favorable to the Tartar raids a protective service alone was maintained. This was called the "Watch and Post Service" and consisted of Cossacks living in rude block- houses linked together by small fortified camps. This first line of defense was intended, however, rather to impede the march of the Tartar raiders – and to give warning of their sudden coming – than to attempt any serious resistance.

Mobile outposts composed of squads of two, four or six horsemen, to each of which was assigned a regular "ride" of about a day's journey, joined together the Cossack encampments or settlements which were generally set upon high places from whence an outlook – could be kept across the plains. In each of these encampments horses stood ready saddled, so that upon the appearance of suspicious signs — the distant black dots in the yellow waste, denoting the scouts of the enemy, or the inevitable clouds of dust raised by the hoofs of their horses the news could be immediately communicated to the nearest fortified town.

The importance of the services thus rendered will be realized when we consider that according to a contemporary English writer — Fletcher — the Tartars of the Crimea Were accustomed to attack the confines of the Muscovite empire in considerable force once or twice every year.

These raids were sometimes carried out at Trinity time, but more often during the harvest season. Now and again a winter raid was undertaken, when the frozen surface of the swamps and rivers facilitated long marches, which only the endurance of the sturdy little Tartar ponies rendered possible. Through constant familiarity with the Russian borderland and the intervening steppes the Tartars learned to know the best trails and bridle tracks, and, most important of all, where the richest booty could most easily be obtained. "Avoiding all river crossings and picking their way along the trackless plateaus — at the same time carefully hiding their movements from the Muscovite steppe riders — they — would suddenly penetrate in a solid mass into some populous district for a distance of about a hundred versts. Then turning in their track and, throwing out long wings to either side of the main body like a flock of wild geese — they would sweep away everything that lay in the path."

Kaffa, in the Crimea, was the principal slave market where the prisoners captured in these raids, men, girls and children, (the latter carefully transported in panniers carried for the purpose) were sold to the Turkish markets.

In protecting the Tsar's dominions against the intolerable suffering caused by these raids, the Cossack became an invaluable adjunct to the armies of the empire. When the Tartars ceased to be a menace a new era of discovery opened to Cossack enterprise; when, after absorbing all neighboring Russian states, the power of the Great Princes of Moscow was turned towards the East in an irresistible movement of expansion which was to extend across Asia to the continent of the New World. Cossack troops played the principal part in these expeditions. Leaders – of whom the Donskoi hetman Yermak was the chief and prototype – crossed Siberia looking for a land passage. An obscure Cossack adventurer engaged in this quest was the first European to set eyes upon the Western coast of the great Alaskan peninsula. Had not the grey waters of the Straits of Behring rolled between – the matchless energy of these frontiersmen might have claimed the western coast of America for the Tsar.

WILLIAM CRESSON

THE ZAPOROGIAN COSSACKS

WHETHER the political condition of the early Cossack settlements of the Ukraine – the wide debatable frontier region lying between Poland, Russia and the Mussulman states to the south and west – ever entitled the *"Free People"* to be considered a separate state or nationality has been a subject of long and fruitless controversy. Matchless frontiersmen, the Cossacks could neither defend nor define the vague boundaries of their own "Free Steppes." At every crisis their undisciplined ways and hatred of a central authority led to internal divisions – and these in turn to inevitable subjection by one of the stronger nations surrounding them.

During the reign of Ivan the Terrible the majority of the Don Cossacks of their own will became subjects of the Russian Tsar while claiming privileges and immunities which have differentiated them from the Russian *moujik* to the present day. The Eastern branch of the Cossack race thus became part of the great Muscovite empire (although they appear to have continued to use the title of "republic" among themselves until a recent date.) During the first half of the sixteenth century the Cossacks inhabiting the shores of the Dnieper, found themselves inevitably drawn into more or less close "alliance" with the Poles against the raids of the

Turks and Tartars. While resisting to the utmost the claims of the Polish magnates, whose vague feudal rights extended over a great part of the lands tilled and defended by the Cossacks, the border *stanitzi* or settlements remained generally subject to the Polish crown.

The kings of Poland soon sought to direct to their own advantage the courage and warlike capacity which their Cossack neighbors had developed through generations of warfare against the common enemy. Under King Sigismond a Cossack *hetman* (called by the Polish chroniclers Ostaphæus) proposed to the Polish Senate that his countrymen be formed into a border guard or militia to defend the frontiers of the kingdom against the Tartars.

His plan contemplated the building of a flotilla on the Dnieper below the cataracts, capable of transporting two thousand men and four hundred horses to any threatened point on the long line of river frontier "which it was necessary to hold against these invaders." He assured the Polish king that even this small force disciplined in Cossack fashion could effectually stop the hordes of the Ghirai Khans of the Crimea, who "were everywhere forced to cross the broad stream by swimming their horses and could thus be taken at a disadvantage."

Under a successor of Ostaphæus, the Hetman Ruchinskov, the Cossacks of the Dneiper in return for a promised subsidy of lands and money from the Polish crown, adopted a method of frontier defense, which later formed the basis of the celebrated military organization of the "Zaporogians." The general plan of this military system in many ways recalls the conditions of modern Cossack military service. To the older men, the weaklings and to the veterans of several campaigns was reserved the privilege of family life in the Cossack settlements or *stanitzi*, scattered along the shores of the upper Dnieper, near Kiev. Here they cultivated the soil and tended the flocks which formed the principal riches of the community.

Meanwhile, the younger men gathered in armed camps and outposts on the islands below the cataracts, ready for any martial adventure that might present itself. These military gatherings, or musters, were especially frequented during the summer months or at any time when hostile raids might be expected. If no foray of the Turks or Tartars threatened the Cossacks' settlements – or the lands of the Polish republic they were paid to defend – expeditions were organized against the Turkish colonies on the shores of the Black Sea. Long Cossack boats, manned by chosen warriors, would then shoot the rapids of the Dnieper, falling with the suddenness of a thunderbolt upon some distant point of the Turkish littoral, even before rumours of their approach could reach the outposts of the enemy.

In winter only the more strategic or threatened points among the islands were fortified and left in charge of a tried garrison consisting of a few thousand men. These chosen troops (called by the Poles *Præsidenti*) were the bands which became famous at a later day under the local name of *Za Porogi* – or men from "beyond the rapids." The principal camp of the Zaporogians protected by outposts and a rude fortress was known as the *sitch*.

The early military organization and strategy of these Dnieper Cossacks was probably but little different from that of the Tartar levies. By the end of the sixteenth century, however, not only the garrisons of the sitch but also the troops and militia stationed in the agricultural settlements along the upper Dnieper, had developed a characteristic system of military service.

In the Hetman Bogdan Kostchinskoi, whose power was recognized by a majority of the free Cossacks settled along the Polish frontiers, King Stephen Bathory found a leader capable of bringing order and discipline out of the anarchy which had previously existed. Upon Bogdan he formally conferred the dignity of "Hetman of the Ukraine" and at the same time presented him with splendid regalia composed of the Asiatic symbols recognized by the Cossacks as those of supreme authority, namely: the *boulava* or baton of the commander- in-chief; the *buntchuk* or horse-tail standard similar to that carried before the conquering generals of Genghis Khan. To these were added the tokens conferred on Polish frontier officials – a great seal of office and the standards that distinguished the mercenaries employed by the kings of Poland.

In the agricultural settlements or *stanitzi* of the Ukraine the Cossack levies were divided into regiments or *polki*. These, in turn, were subdivided into companies of one hundred men called *sotnia*, an organization which has persisted in the Cossack forces of the present day. Although a general of artillery, or *obozni* and a secretary, or *pisari* were nominated by the Polish king to assist the hetman (and at the same time to oversee the more technical details of military organisation) the warlike customs of the Cossacks were not interfered with and their peculiar methods of fighting and discipline were generally maintained. Desirous at first of building up the strength of the Cossack class, the Polish nobles allowed these tribesmen to extend their homesteads and settlements into southern Podolia and Volhynia, permitting them to enroll as "Free Cossacks" all of the fugitive Russian serfs and other strangers who succeeded in joining their forces. By this wise policy Bathory intended to interpose between the frontiers of Poland and the rising power of Russia a military state or province devoted to the interests of the elective kingdom. At the same time, by bringing into cultivation the rich steppes of the Ukraine which had lain desolate for so many centuries through fear of the Tartar raiders, he opened new channels for the commerce of the Polish cities. That these wise plans were not destined to be fully realized was due to several causes difficult to foresee.

In considering the history of the Ukraine, a distinction must be made between the agricultural Cossack settlements of the Upper Dnieper and the outposts or garrisons of the " *Za-Porogi*" to which the former were tributary. The cataracts of the Lower Dnieper are divided just below the modern city of Ekaterinoslav by an archipelago of hundreds of rocky islands covered with a shaggy growth of stunted timber and underbrush. To navigate the secret channels of this watery labyrinth requires rare skill with the paddle, a knowledge to be obtained only through constant familiarity. By throwing up a few entrenchments of logs and earthworks any of these islands, isolated by the rapids, was capable of offering an almost impregnable defense against the attacks of an army not supplied with artillery.

The principal camp or *sitch* of the Cossack garrison was established on one of the larger islands, or at some inaccessible point on the river. This main camp was, moreover, frequently transferred from one place to another so that the mystery which surrounded its location hid the varying numbers of its garrison and added to the difficulties of attack.

The military capabilities and peculiar organization of the Zaporogian Cossacks was a source of considerable interest and inquiry among contemporary military authorities. Many writers of the eighteenth century – wholly ignorant of their real condition – compared these famous frontier troops to military orders of chivalry such as the Knights of the Sword in Lithuania, or even the Knights of Malta. Others compared them to the "Free Archers" of Charles the Seventh, or the "military colonies" of Sparta and of the early Grecian states. As Lesur points out, a more reasonable and modern parallel is to be found in that strange republic of *filibusters* who almost contemporaneously established their piratical state among the islands of the West Indies. If this comparison does some injustice to the Zaporogians (to whom must be allowed the merit of holding in check, at a critical time, the ravages of the Mussulman invaders) it will appear more reasonable if viewed in the light of the intolerable nuisance to which their pretensions gave rise at a later date. For, while the Cossack settlements, as we shall presently see, became in the course of time absorbed by the civilization of their Russian neighbours, the "Free Companions" of the *sitch* refused to adapt themselves in any way to the new modes of life made necessary by the passing of frontier conditions.

Long after their territory had become surrounded by peaceful agricultural colonists, the Zaporogians continued to live their own boisterous life as in the days when the Tartar raids almost hourly threatened the community. As far as the author is aware, no historian has ever attempted to trace the development of the crude system of island outposts until these became merged in the famous military brotherhood of the semi-independent Zaporogians, or, as they generally styled themselves, "The Free and Independent Community Beyond the Rapids." Nevertheless, the history of the long struggle between Poland and Russia for the fertile provinces of the Ukraine is very largely concerned with the doings of this turbulent faction among the Cossack "nation." To form a true idea of the appearance of the famous *sitch* or stronghold one must imagine rather an encampment or gathering of rude huts set down amidst a clearing in the forest. These were defended by the rapids of the Dnieper, or by rude earthworks in no way recalling a mediæval fortress. Great sheds or barracks built of saplings, covered with horse or cow-hides, sheltered the garrison and divided it into definite units or *kourens*. The members of each *kouren* sleeping under one roof, eating their *kasha* or buckwheat meal from a single great kettle, enjoyed in common a kind of boisterous family life. In spite of the iron discipline which their exposed and dangerous position rendered necessary, the government of the *sitch* was jealously maintained on the most democratic lines. The chief of this warlike republic was known as the *koshovoy ataman*. Although possessed of almost unlimited powers, this officer was liable at any moment to be deposed from his high position by a public meeting of the brotherhood. These assemblies were called together by the most informal means – the clashing of cymbals or the tumultuous cries of any party strong enough to rouse the general interests. Together with his aide-de-camp or *jessoul* and his *clerk*, or *pissar*, the koshovoy ataman might thus be summoned on the most frivolous pretext to stand before the assembled garrison. Taking his station beneath the horsetail standard that denoted his rank, he was expected to wait, cap in hand, the outcome of the noisy debate which decided whether or not his administration was satisfactory to the Free Companions. The ceremony just described was generally preceded by a drinking bout wherein quantities of *gorilka*, brandy (with which the hardy warriors braced themselves when called upon to make any momentous decision), were consumed as a necessary preliminary to the mental effort required. It is, therefore, not surprising to learn that such elections, more often than not, ended in bloodshed.

Whenever the tumult seemed to indicate that their services were no longer required, it was the custom of the officials composing an unpopular "administration" formally to salute their comrades, and clapping on their shaggy sheepskin headgear, to return to the ranks of their own *kouren* thus resuming their rights as Free Cossacks.

"The election of a new *koshovoy ataman* then proceeded under conditions which made the acceptance of this high honour as humiliating as possible for the successful candidate. The *kouren* from which the *ataman* was to be chosen having first been decided upon, an individual member was next singled out by the noisy shouts of his adherents. Ten of the most insolent and intoxicated elders of the general assembly were usually deputed to announce to the new chieftain the honour conferred upon him. It was no false modesty that often caused the responsibilities of this high position to be declined. Like Cæsar, etiquette demanded that the newly elected *koshovoy* should at least twice refuse the dangerous distinction offered him. It was only after being knocked half senseless by the back slapping and rough congratulations of his electors that he might properly consent to be dragged beneath the red horsetail standard where the final indignity connected with his installation awaited him. The oldest Cossacks present, gathering up handfuls of mud from the river bank, proceeded in turn to smear with this filth the beard and face of their newly-chosen leader. In this condition he was obliged – though now enjoying the dignity of remaining covered before the uncapped assembly – to make a long speech thanking his comrades for the honours literally thrust upon him. As additional safeguard to the democratic institutions of the Zaporogians, it was further decreed (by laws none the less binding because only part of the unwritten traditions of the community) that except during an active campaign the *koshovoy ataman* should exercise no real authority in the sitch. When, however, war had once been declared, even his most despotic commands were implicitly obeyed.

In ordinary times the administration of the affairs of the Zaporogian *sitch* lay in the hands of a council of subordinate *atamans* elected by the different *kourens*. These were generally selected from among the most popular members of the community and only kept themselves in office by exercising arts of the basest flattery and slavish generosity. No *ataman* might receive any pay, except the privilege of renting stalls to the Jews and other traders venturesome enough to establish themselves among the Zaporogians. Commerce was held in so little esteem that nearly all human rights were denied these despised shopkeepers. Any moment might see their stock in trade looted before their eyes, yet the high prices which after some successful raid the Cossacks were liable to toss to the "peddlers" rather than demean themselves by bargaining, always attracted a motley crowd of vendors willing to submit to all the humiliations which might be heaped upon them in return for the rich profits to be gained. Although these periods of iron discipline and the relaxations of ensuing debauch were characteristic of the life of the *sitch*, contemporary writers give the Zaporogians credit for certain homely virtues. They were always honest with each other. Convicted thieves were treated with cruel severity: lashed to a post in the centre of the camp, if they or their friends were unable to make restitution at the end of a period of three days, they might be beaten to death by their victims. The murderer of a comrade was chained to his victim's corpse and buried alive in the same grave. But besides these cruel laws born of the necessities of early times, there grew up a more civilized code based upon the celebrated medieval "Institutes of Magdeburg," – regulations which were applied in the merchants' quarters of the Polish towns.

A custom of the *sitch* doubtless growing out of the dangers constantly threatening the first garrisons and the state of constant watchfulness and alarm in which they were forced to live, has gained no little attention from contemporary writers. This was the law rigorously excluding women, under pain of death, from the community of the Zaporogians. If a Zaporogian desired to take up the burdens and pleasures of family life he returned to the Cossack settlements, while his name was inexorably erased from the rolls of the Free Company. From the accounts of this custom many ludicrous errors have arisen. Some writers have described the Zaporogians as a kind of monkish militia, constantly at war with the infidels in the defense of Christianity. Others have described them as a religious order of chivalry with vows of chastity resembling those taken by the Knights of the Sword, who ruled in Lithuania.

Although any parade of piety seems strangely out of place in such a rough community, it was considered necessary for each new recruit to belong to the Orthodox Greek religion. Matters of doctrine, we read, were the cause of many bloody quarrels among them. Every year two priests and their attendant deacons were sent from a monastery near Kiev to the encampment charged with celebrating a daily mass. "A deep bass voice and ability to drink a fair share of Cossack brandy" were, according to Lesur, considered part of the necessary equipment for ministering to the spiritual needs of this strange parish. In the face of the fanatical religious zeal of the Turks and Tartars the Zaporogians could hardly allow themselves to be outdone in this respect. To the battle cry of "Allah! Allah!" the Zaporogians answered with the rallying cry of "Jesus!" On the banners of these strange crusaders were emblazoned the symbols of favourite saints and martyrs of the Ukraine. Their feuds with the Turkish colonies established on the Black Sea, were embittered by religious hatred as well as love of plunder. In their fragile river craft they set out fearlessly across the Black Sea in reckless forays against the Turk: protecting the low sides of their canoes in stormy weather by mats made of reeds, or else by lashing their boats together to form catamarans. These typical Cossack boats, or *cholni*, were often sixty feet in length. They were built in shipyards hidden among the reedy islands of the lower Dnieper by skilful artisans held in high respect among Zaporogians. Often as many as fifteen oars on a side were manned by

Cossack rowers, while a small cannon was set on a platform at the prow. On account of their size and "handiness" the Cossack "navy" was capable of disconcerting manœuvres unknown to Turkish strategy, so that even the great war galleys of the "All-conquering" Sultan Murad fell victims to their attack.

These exploits, for which enthusiastic volunteers were never lacking, kept up the military spirit and discipline of the Zaporogians. Whenever a short peace with the Tartars of the Crimea (the foe with which they were most concerned) permitted such relaxations, some chieftain was always ready to lead an expedition against the Sultan. Even when their allies were at peace with the Porte, it was impossible to prevent these raids on the "Land of the Infidel." In order to avoid unnecessary quarrels, it was only after returning to the sitch that the division of the booty took place. On such occasions the whole community would indulge in a huge masquerade. Their usual rough and tattered garments were then replaced with silken Turldsh cloaks and the costly velvet cloths of Damascus. Rich damasks were ruthlessly cut up to make *zippoun*, the characteristic trousers of portentous width affected by all true Cossacks of the old school. Thus arrayed and with their shaggy calpacks, decorated with ostrich feathers and jewelled aigrets, the Cossacks would march in procession to pay their respects to the neighboring settlements, forcing all whom they met upon the road to drink with them – Polish nobles or Cossack peasants alike. "Four or five days were spent in drinking, dancing and boastful discourses. Everywhere the Cossacks were accompanied by a rude orchestra and by serving men bearing huge jars of beer, hydromel () and Cossack brandy. Thus, at the end of a few days all the profits of their perilous expeditions would be dissipated."

*

HISTORY OF THE COSSACKS

When after the Cossack revolution led by Bogdan Hmielnicki, the principal Cossack settlements of the Ukraine passed under the Russian rule, it became apparent (especially after the rise of the Romanov dynasty) that there was no place for such an aggressively independent community as that of the Zaporogians within the borders of the Empire ruled by the Tsar. Unlike the loosely held frontiers of the Polish kingdom, the Russian marches were guarded by imperial troops. Yet the remoteness of the Cossack settlements and the position occupied by the *sitch*, preserved for a century or more the "national" pretensions of the Zaporogians. But the later history of this warlike brotherhood presents only a series of episodes without signs of political development or progress. The rare documents of this period, preserved in the convents of the Ukraine, are records of achievements startling in their bravery, sometimes chivalrous, but often base and cruel. The love of personal freedom, at a time when their neighbours were bound in shameful subjection, alone gives character and unity to their story.

An attempt will now be made to give, in the language and spirit of the original report (made to the Ataman Dorochenko by the great Zaporogian *koshevoy* Sirko), some account of a famous foray of the "Free Companions" against the Crimean Tartars and their allies. This document may be taken as a typical example of the rare "sources" of Cossack history which have survived to the present day – although the golden days of the *sitch* at the close of the seventeenth century and the beginning of the eighteenth were probably filled with episodes similar to the one described. The author has resisted all temptation (in the interest of "historical truth") to tamper with the characteristic bombast which marks the original. These rare written records of Cossack days and the joyous "diplomatic" correspondence which accompanies them are, moreover, of especial interest as having suggested to the great Russian historical painter Repnin, the subject for his well-known Cossack pictures in the Tretiakov Gallery of Moscow.

*

"It was only when the Dnieper was filled with floating ice floes, and the steppes covered with soft snow that the ever-vigilant Cossack garrison of the *sitch* could feel themselves in a measure safe from the attacks of their implacable enemies, the Tartars of the Crimea. During this season the fast of St. Phillip, which occurs shortly before Christmas, was always strictly kept by the members of the orthodox Zaporogian brotherhood. Following this period of abstinence, if the weather and the conditions of the plains afforded their usual protection, it was an equally honoured custom for the Cossacks to indulge in a period of feasting and drunkenness."

In the year 1675, profiting by intimate knowledge of their habits gained by many years of warfare, the Khan of the Crimea determined to attack the community of the sitch at this time. Turkish troops had been loaned to the Khan of the Crimea by the Turkish Sultan for reinforcements and a serious attempt was to be made to put an end to the depredation of the Cossacks in Turkish territory.

By following the course of the Dnieper, yet remaining at a distance of several miles from its frozen banks, the vigilance of the Cossack patrols was avoided and a large force of Crimean Tartars and Turkish Janissaries reached the neighbourhood of the Zaporogian encampment unnoticed by its defenders.

In judging of the numbers which composed this important expedition, we can only depend on the evidence in the Cossack accounts. Let us then state, once for all, that (if the worthy Cossack *pissar* or clerk can be believed) "on one side were engaged no less than 15,000 Janissaries or regular Turkish troops," besides a "multitude" of Tartar tribesmen, while the usual winter garrison of the sitch did not, as a rule, exceed 2,000 men.

On arriving at a spot nearly opposite the island fortress occupied by the Zaporogians, the "perfidious" Mussulmen had the good fortune to find the entire Cossack outpost guarding this important point overcome by their libations in honour of the "Holy Day" preceding. (The Cossack historian, in strong and convincing language here sets forth the iniquity of an attack made at such a time!!) Through the "base advantage" thus gained nearly the entire force of Janissaries and "numerous" Tartars were enabled actually to penetrate undiscovered within the narrow streets of the encampment where they proceeded to surround each of the *kouren*, or wooden barracks, in which the Cossack companies were housed. It was at this juncture that their presence was made known to the garrison by a Cossack named Chefchika who, "moved by God" chanced to glance out of a window and, by the light reflected from the snow, saw to his "grim amazement," the silent ranks of the enemy drawn up and awaiting the signal to attack.

His courage in no way affected by this sight, he proceeded quietly to awaken his sleeping comrades. It was determined that the best method of meeting the attack would be to place at the few available windows the most skilful of the Cossack marksmen, while the others should load and pass to them guns and pistols in rapid succession. This system of defense in which the other *kourens* presently joined, was apparently so disconcerting to the Turkish troops, that when the gallant defenders sallied out for a final assault they found only a demoralized mob of the enemy upon whom to wreak their vengeance.

*

Following the example of the Cossack historian we shall pass over the minor tactical details of the struggle which ensued, confining ourselves to the glorious outcome. The results of this indiscreet invasion, according to the chronicler, was a "loss of no less than 13,500 men among the Janissaries alone, while on the Cossack side a loss of but fifty killed is recorded, besides eighty wounded" (sic). The first pious duty of the Cossacks was to bury their own dead in consecrated ground, while the wounded were given over "to the care of the barber." In the meantime some two thousand cavalrymen started out in pursuit of the Khan of Crimea, who, on the defeat of his Turkish allies, had "fled like a wolf" to his distant stronghold. To judge by the account we have quoted, one of the principal "annoyances" caused by this invasion was the question of how to dispose of the numerous bodies, of slain Tartars and Janissaries, which encumbered the streets of the Cossack encampment. These, after much discussion (recorded at even greater length in the original manuscript than the account of the actual fighting itself) were pushed under the ice of the river Dnieper through holes laboriously cut for that purpose, whence they were swept away by the swift current.

The "facts" contained in the above short summary are at least borne out by the tone of the correspondence which ensued between the Zaporogian Cossacks and the Turkish Sultan, whose disloyal actions during a time of peace had been so signally punished. One letter reads as follows: "*To the Khan of Tartary Our Unworthy Neighbour*:

We, the Cossack troops of the *sitch*, would never have conceived the idea of entering upon this war had you not commenced hostilities. You have sent against us (what treachery!) not only your savage Tartars, but also the troops of that old fool, the Sultan. Had it not been for the intervention of our constant friend, the great Lord Jesus – we might all have perished in our sleep! Now, since your disloyal ways have brought upon you disaster — refrain from troubling us. Otherwise, we will treat you after our fashion, and that of our noble Cossack ancestors, by beating down your own gates!

We wish your Majesty a long and prosperous reign.

Signed by IVAN SIRKO, — Koshovoy Ataman *(for the whole community)*."

At the same time a letter was written to the Sultan in Constantinople, Mahmoud III — beginning with a parody of his imperial titles as set forth at the beginning of a letter admonishing the Cossacks to keep the peace. The epithets show a cunning knowledge of what would be most insulting to a pious Moslem.

"*Thou Turkish Devil:*

Brother and Companion of Lucifer himself! Who dares call himself Lord of the Christians — but is not! Babylonish cook! Brewer of Jerusalem! Goat-keeper of the herds of Alexandria! Swineherd of Great and Lesser Egypt! Armenian Sow and Tartar Goat! Insolent Unbeliever! May the Devil Take you! The Cossacks refuse every demand and petition that you now make to them — or that you may in future invent. Thank us for condescending to answer you!

(Signed) IVAN SIRKO *and the Cossack troops*."

The originals of the above epistles, which, for obvious reasons, have been considerably condensed and modified, are to be found in the annals of Kiev, Vol. II, pp. 371, 382, 1891. See also a pamphlet published in Petrograd in 1902 by Professor I. Evamitzky.

WILLIAM CRESSON

YERMAK AND THE COSSACK CONQUEST OF SIBERIA

ACCORDING to Lesur, the French historian (who, at Napoleon's bidding, wrote a careful and erudite *"History of the Cossacks"*) it was the singular destiny of the Hetman Yermak and his Donskoi followers to add the immense empire of Siberia to the Russian crown, rather by chance than through any deliberate plan of discovery or conquest. In the course of an attempt to escape the vengeance they had incurred by breaking the stern peace declared along the Volga by Ivan the Terrible, this band of marauding Cossacks were cut off by the Tsar's forces from access to the "Free Steppes" and obliged to ascend the course of the mighty river towards the unknown North. Here Yermak repeated among the aborigines of the Arctic, exploits only comparable with the adventures met with a generation before by Pizarro during his conquest of Peru.

The vast land known as Siberia covers nearly one-quarter of the habitable globe. Until the latter half of the fifteenth century this great expanse of territory was as unknown to Europe as the trackless ocean crossed by Columbus. About the time that the continent of America was discovered the Russians first entered into relations with what was then called the land of "Iougra," the wide "back country" beyond the low chain of the Urals. Upon the savage tribes of this borderland the free burghers of "Lord Novgorod the Great" laid a tribute of skins and precious metals.

In an ill-chosen moment — just after the conquest of Kazan (1556) and before Ivan the Terrible had disbanded his victorious troops — a Siberian prince named Iadiger attempted to evade the promised yearly tax formerly paid to the republic of Novgorod, whose liberties the Tsars of Moscow had trampled underfoot but a short time before. The loss of the tribute, paid by the thirty thousand subjects of the Siberian princeling, — which had been set at a "marten skin per inhabitant," — directed the attention of the redoubtable Tsar towards the resources of the vast unknown territories to the eastward of his empire.

In the district of Oustioug, north of Viatka, a family of Russian *boyars* of Tartar origin, the Stroganovs, had for several generations exploited salt and iron mines. Although belonging to the merchant class, an exception seems to have been made in their favour from the rigid policy of celltralization adopted by the princes of Moscow. The Stroganovs not only exercised "the rights of High Justice and Low," but were also allowed to maintain an armed force, on a footing which prepared them either for trade or war with the neigbbouring Siberian chieftains. Their venture appears to have prospered, for, in 1558, Anakievitch Stroganov (according to records preserved in Moscow), petitioned Ivan the Terrible for a "further concession of 106 square versts on the shores of the Kama" where he proposed "to erect a fort against the Tartars." At this place in the year 1579 a band of 640 Cossacks suddenly appeared desiring to be enrolled in the private army of the Stroganovs. These adventurers were under the double leadership of a Cossack named Ivan Koltso (who, accordcording to some authorities, had not long before been condemned to ignominious death by the Tsar's orders), and a hardly more reputable *hetman* named Yermak. The name of the latter, preserved in stirring popular ballads and *bylines*, was later to typify the pioneering and imperialistic genius of the Russian race. Whether the legendary exploits of this illustrious brigand represent the actual history of an individual, or whether, as some Russian historians maintain, we have in Yermak one of those composite heroes to the making of whose reputation the fame of half a score of lesser pioneers has been sacrificed, is a fact impossible to verify at the present day.

Aside from their sudden and suspicious appearance in the district administered by the Stroganovs, all that was known of Yermak and his Cossack companions can hardly have induced these prosperous merchants to invite the newcomers to remain longer than necessary in the vicinity of their warehouses filled with stores of precious furs and metals. During the dark winter months following their arrival, the merchants appear to have urged upon their guests the glorious advantages to be gained by a campaign against the forest tribes, whose villages and hunting grounds lay just beyond this frontier station. In proof of these statements they showed the eager Cossacks nuggets of placer gold and specimens of those strangely coloured, semi-precious minerals of the Urals which even modern geologists are often at a loss to value or classify. Among the Voguls, Ostiaks and other peoples of Finnish origin against whom the Stroganovs had for generations carried on their indecisive forays, the Cossacks were assured that gold was "hardly prized at all." Other booty, it was urged, such as furs and mastodon ivory, might readily be captured from such cowardly and ill-armed forces. It is, moreover, probable that the Cossack leaders (at least one of whom still felt a noose tickling his neck) were only too glad of an excuse to put further leagues of wilderness between the avenging troops of Ivan the Terrible and their own guilty persons.

Unknown to Yermak at this time, his most heroic contest was to be waged with the natural difficulties of the wilderness. Such a struggle was less suitable, perhaps, for the poetic treatment of the *bylines* than his battles with the aborigines. But any traveller who has had occasion to visit the country lying about the Urals Will find, in the Cossack leader's persistent courage as an explorer, a subject of admiration which will out-rival his military achievements. The native tribes they first encountered – unlike the more warlike subjects of the Tartar princes further to the southward – could not oppose any formidable resistance to the better armed Cossacks. Like the scattered remnants of their descendants who survive to the present day, the Voguls and Ostiaks lived in family groups dispersed in the deepest recesses of the forest. They were small of stature, cowardly and anxious to live at peace with their neighbours. In addition to the real dangers of the wilderness they inhabited, a thousand other foolish terrors assailed them through their superstitious belief in forest demons, wood sprites and other fantastic creatures, whom they propitiated by a system of complicated idolatrous rites. These beliefs forming their only religion led them to look upon their chiefs or medicine men with uncanny reverence.

Skilful hunters and trappers – so that their filthy bodies were covered with the rare furs of mink, otter and royal ermine – their only weapons of defense were bows and arrows. Against such adversaries the firearms of the Cossacks, like those carried by the *conquistadores* of Peru, were quick to establish a terrible superiority.

The almost impenetrable forest through which Yermak and his followers were forced step by step, to cut their way, the swollen streams dashing towards the Arctic Sea, across which they were obliged to pass, and the deep ravines filled with chevaux de frises of fallen timber, were the difficulties which at first combined – rather than the feeble though growing resistance of the native tribes – to impede the eastward march of the Cossacks. Indeed the short northern summer was wholly passed in contending with these natural obstacles, and Yermak realized the necessity of returning once more to his winter quarters with the Stroganovs. To the latter this second winter's visit must have been even less welcome than the first. Nor did the diplomatic merchants cease their efforts to encourage the Cossacks to persist in their adventure of looking for a practicable pathway toward the unknown riches in the "beyond."

When the second slow-coming springtime had arrived Yermak had succeeded in enforcing a system of rigid military discipline among his unruly followers. Attempts at desertion, or disobedience of orders were punished by cruel penalties. According to Lesur, the crime of blasphemy was one of those most pitilessly forbidden. By Yermak's orders a portable altar with an ikon of St. Nicholas "the Wonder-Worker" was constructed to accompany the little army during its second expedition and before the Holy Ikons a renegade monk, assisted by two unfrocked priests, regularly celebrated a forest mass on Sundays and Holy Days.

The delays of the second winter also enabled the Cossacks to fit themselves out with a little train of portable artillery whose strange thunders (and the terrifying clouds of thick smoke given off by the coarse gunpowder manufactured by the Stroganovs) doubled its effectiveness against the savage enemy.

The Stroganovs, by exciting the cupidity and ambition of the Cossacks simplified the task of their leader. Tales of the riches awaiting them, once the forest-guarded mountain chain of the Urals could be crossed, were eagerly listened to during the long winter nights of enforced idleness. Thus, from an undisciplined band of brigands and ruffians Yermak's genius for leadership welded a small but highly tempered little army capable of resisting the hardships they were to encounter for the second time.

Yet the end of a second summer's campaign found Yermak only a little farther advanced than at the end of the previous year. On the banks of the Ka or Silver River (a stream which has since become famous for its fisheries) he decided to pass the winter in an entrenched camp. This enabled him, in spite of terrible sufferings from the cold, to push on with the first signs of spring, his route following the course of the river Toura.

Until this point had been reached the principal difficulties met with on Yermak's line of march were the natural obstacles and the problem of obtaining provisions. But the expedition now found itself confronted by more valiant enemies. The Tartar and Tartar-led tribes along the shores of the stream they were obliged to follow offered a stubborn and unexpected resistance. The whole summer was consumed in bitter skirmishes with this new enemy (1580).

The third long northern winter was passed in the little town of Tchingis, near the modern city of Tioumen. The Tartar inhabitants of this place had amassed a considerable store of grain, and possessed besides, flocks of sheep and cattle, so that for the Cossacks the winter passed pleasantly enough. Spring found them descending the swollen Toura (seeking to gain the course of a stream now recognized as the Tobol, whose waters were reported to be navigable) and here Yermak and his followers encountered for the first time an army formidable in numbers and equipment. No less than six confederated Tartar chieftains gathering their subject Vogul and Ostiak tribesmen, awaited the coming of the Cossacks in an easily defendable pass. Fortunately the latter were now able to build and launch upon the lower Toura the "long boats" which many of their number had learned to manoeuvre with skill among the rocks and rapids of the

HISTORY OF THE COSSACKS

Dneiper.

The forces of the enemy, defending every rocky pass and difficult portage, though again and again dispersed, returned with fresh re-enforcements to dispute the way. The more faint-hearted among the Cossacks even began to talk of returning to Russia. But Yermak could now afford to peer at the protests of these malcontents. The intrepid leader at last possessed an unanswerable argument: pointing out the impossibility of returning against the current of the long rapids that lay behind them. In their dismal councils even the mutineers decided that the only safety lay in pressing forward towards the unknown.

We now come to an incident in Yermak's voyage made famous by the Russian ballad singers — the telling of which never fails to draw a shout of laughter from their hearers. In the peasant *izbas* of the North or the Cossack villages of the Ukraine, the cleverly planned ruse invented by the hero Yermak to disengage his men from the ambuscade laid by the Tartars and Voguls is always a favourite incident of folk-history. At a place where the little Cossack army was forced to pass through a long fall of rapids (a point where the Tobol rushes between high narrow banks) the Tartars had raised a barrier of rocks and logs "clamped together with iron chains," meanwhile entrenching themselves on the overhanging cliffs along the shore. With their little flotilla rushing headlong towards this well-laid trap, Yermak and his men learned of its existence in the nick of time. Some urged the leader to abandon the boats — built with so much toil and indispensable for the further success of their journey — and by proceeding across country to avoid the Tartar entrenchments. But the master-cunning of Yermak was equal to the occasion. By his orders short lengths of logs were cut and set up in the "long boats." These he draped with the tattered uniforms of his followers, while each scarecrow figure, surmounted with a shaggy Cossack *calpack*, was provided with a long sapling to simulate the Cossack pikes. Upon these dummy warriors, steering down upon them during the evening dusk, – each boat guided by one brave volunteer – the Tartar hordes loosed the fury of their bows and arrows. What must have been their dismay to find themselves in turn surprised and overwhelmed by a new army – the nearly naked forces of Yermak, who, creeping cautiously through the bushes attacked them fiercely from the flank and rear.

Soon after this event news was brought to Yermak that near Karatchin, a little town not far from the river Ob, a Tartar prince had gathered and bidden a "great treasure" which included, besides a store of native placer gold and precious stones, a part of the spoil captured by the soldiers of Genghis Khan. (These were treasures, which the soldiers of the great Asiatic conqueror were carrying back with them to Tartary, when, as the chroniclers state "they fell into the hands of the even more barbarous Voguls.") Yermak now harangued his followers concerning the merit to be obtained in recovering from the heathen these sacred vessels of gold and silver robbed from the churches and monasteries of Holy Russia.

Decided by Yermak's persuasions to turn aside from their journey in order to undertake this pious adventure, the conquest proved an easy one for the Cossacks. But the added weight of their spoil nearly proved the undoing of these strange crusaders. Again, in reading the story of Yermak's exploits we are reminded of the conquistadores Pizarro and Alvarado in the bleak Andean highlands, who although starving, clung to the golden spoils of the Peruvian Incas until they fell exhausted by the way. But the courage of the Cossack army was now strengthened by tangible proofs that this bleak wilderness actually concealed riches and booty – a tithe at least of that promised them by the Stroganovs.

In their retreat the Tartars had diligently swept the entire countryside bare of provisions, but Yermak meets each new danger with another ruse: the solemn Fast of the Assumption being at hand, instead of the fourteen days of fasting prescribed by the Russian ritual, the resourceful Cossack leader declares a "fast of repentance" lasting forty days. Thus even the cruel hunger tearing at their vitals renewed – through their mystical faith – the strength of his little army. No less sustaining, perhaps, was the hope of yet richer spoils through the sack of the Tartar cities which they knew lay just beyond.

*

Ever true to the unities of a great epic the crisis of our chronicle now approaches. The Kalmouck Prince Koutzum, of the imperial Tartar house of Timour Mangou Khan, at this time ruled over all the country between the river Ob and the Urals. To his exalted leadership even the rebellious Samoyeds, Voguls and Ostiaks now submitted in the face of the common danger. His woodland capital, protected by staked palisades and surrounded by a deep moat, was established at a place called Ishir, which, as the ballad-chronicle states, "the Europeans called Sibir." The site of this forest metropolis (which may have given its name to the whole vast territory of Siberia) was not far from the present city of Tobolsk. Here was to occur the inevitable meeting of those whom the *bylines* call the "lords of the future and of the past."

The battle, long expected and apparently equally dreaded by both sides, was decided in favour of the Cossacks by a curious incident. A Russian cannon which during some foray with the Tartars had fallen into the hands of the forest tribesmen, had for generations been revered as a redoubtable fetish by the Voguls. Dragging this silent weapon with them to the battle field, the savages confidently turned it upon the attack of Yermak's little army – which was advancing upon them in a dense mass, the thunderbolts of the dreaded firearms playing like lightning along its front. But heedless of the incantations of the *shamans* the weapon in which the Voguls had placed their hopes remained obstinately silent. Their fatuous belief in its magical powers had led them to expect their ordinance to vomit destruction of its own accord upon their enemies! Thus betrayed in their dearest hopes they turned and fled into their impenetrable forests – leaving their Tartar allies to bear the brunt of the Cossack charge.

Terribly reduced in numbers, the Cossack forces probably consisted at this time of but little more than three hundred men, while aside from the undependable woodlanders, the Tartar-trained warriors among the enemy were hardly more numerous. It would thus appear that the fate of the great Siberian empire hung on the fortunes of what was little more than a woodland skirmish!

This decisive victory, won over the acknowledged chief of the Trans-Ural, and the valuable spoil gained in the encounter, encouraged Yermak to take a momentous step. He now decided to enter into negotiations with the distant court of Ivan the Terrible, and to secure a pardon from his sovereign if possible for all past misdeeds. That Yermak (who had now advanced into an unknown country beyond the reach of the Tsar's justice, and occupied a position comparable to that of an independent prince) should thus trembling seek to make his peace with the distant ruler in Moscow, is a sign of the great progress towards national unity which Russia had made under the stern rule of the Tsar Vasili and his successor. The spectacle of a Spanish *hidalgo*, all powerful in his colonial realm, ordering himself home to execution or to await the pleasure of his king, had already been noted on more than one occasion in the chronicles of Spanish-

America. In Russia, however, such conduct is the mark of a new era.

But even in making his doubtful peace with Ivan, Yermak was cautious. Either doubtful of his own reception, or anxious to maintain his recent conquests, he ordered his lieutenant, Koltso (who apparently now occupied a wholly subordinate position) to undertake this task. A condemned criminal, with a price upon his head, thus became the messenger chosen to announce to Ivan that a vast new territory, which Cossack courage had conquered, had been added to his empire.

Here, again, the poetic version of the folksongs which have built up the popular legend of Yermak, and the records of history are wholly in accord. Ivan, after listening with interest to the tale of Yermak's adventures, readily forgave Koltso and his companions. Graciously accepting the "sixty sacks of precious furs" (which the Cossack artfully represented were but the first tribute of a conquered nation) he promised to take Siberia under his "protection." In return, Koltso was charged to deliver to Yermak, besides the cloak which the Tsar wore upon his own august shoulders, a magnificent cuirass, destined to play a fatal rôle in the fast approaching climax of Yermak's legendary career.

An even more acceptable favour was the prompt dispatch of five hundred troops from Ivan's new army who were sent to reinforce Yermak's depleted forces. These were placed under the temporary command of Prince Volkowski, a *dvorianin*, or courtier from the imperial court. As a further honour, "they were enrolled under the title of *Cossacks*, heretofore no very complimentary appellation in the eyes of constituted Russian authority." Moreover, the supreme command of the expedition appears to have remained in Yermak's hands in spite of the presence of the imperial representative.

*

But the long epic of Yermak's adventures now nears its close. The winter following the safe return from Moscow of Koltso accompanied by the Russian voevod, had been a disastrous one for the Cossacks. The supply of food upon which the expedition depended for the cold season was exhausted long before spring, perhaps through the unexpected arrival of new reinforcements. Much valuable provender had been burned or wasted in brutal unnecessary forays against the villages of the forest tribesmen. Even the flight of the latter was fatal to their conquerors. The Voguls and Ostiaks possessed secrets and "charms" unknown to the Cossacks for capturing the winter game and for fishing during the season when the ice upon the rivers was too thick to cut through. Thus, through their own misdeeds famine and a great pestilence broke out among the Cossacks. Among the first to succumb was the *dvorianin*, the imperial courtier commanding Ivan's troops.

Learning of these misfortunes the enemy now began to gather in formidable numbers and often boldly attacked the Cossack camp. Koltso, Yermak's fellow leader, was ambushed and slain during a foray in search of provisions.

Following this series of disasters the welcome news was brought to Yermak that a caravan of Bokhariot merchants had arrived from Central Asia to trade with the new Russian outposts. This important mission, it was reported, had been halted through fear of meeting Koutzum's Tartar soldiers on the shores of the Vagai, an affluent of the Irtish. The Cossacks now decided to go boldly forth to protect the march of the caravan towards their camp. Too late they learned that they had been made the victims of a Tartar ruse. Yermak and his men, surrounded on all sides in a woodland ambush, took refuge on an island in the Irtish. Here, while the whole camp slept exhausted by the privations of their march, they were surprised by the enemy. Yermak, at the head of a trusted handful of his followers, cut his way with little difficulty through the ranks of the enemy, who no longer dared to meet the hero face to face. Then, while making good his retreat, a false step threw the Cossack leader into the swift, deep current of the stream. The weight of his rich cuirass, the fatal gift of the Tsar, from which, with superstitious reverence, he never had separated himself, pinned him among the stones at the bottom of the river.

The Apotheosis: Here the sober thread of probability in the narrative of Yermak becomes almost lost in the bright legends which the *bylines* have woven about the hero's end.

"The Tartars, recognizing the body of the chieftain by the great golden eagle emblazoned on his armor, hung the corpse upon a framework of poles, and for six weeks made it a target for their archers. Yet even the carrion birds of prey, wheeling in the dark clouds about the hero's head, respected the august remains – a terrifying and prodigious proof to the Mussulmen that the dead leader was of no common clay! At night a cloud of baleful fire flickered about his head . . .," and this although no odor of putrefaction arose from the body!" The Tartars, persuaded by these omens, decided to bury the remains of Yermak with all the ceremony due to one of their own heroes. His grave, for many generations, became the resort of the Tartar magicians and of the *shamans* or "Medicine-men" who were most honoured among the Voguls and Ostiaks . . . ." Thus bereft in turn of their three leaders, the Cossack expedition returned in disorder to the Russian outposts. For a time the conquests that Yermak had made with so much courage and persistence were abandoned. But his discoveries and example had not been in vain. The legend of the Cossack hero – an epic of empire

— remained to stir the Cossack spirit to new adventures. It was largely through Cossack exploration and settlement that the vast land of Siberia was made known to Europe during the two succeeding centuries.

In a recent work by Prof. Golder, the eminent American authority on the history of Alaska, the story of the discovery of and explorations in Eastern Siberia and the Western coast of America by Yermak's successors is told in fascinating detail.

Upon his deathbed Peter the Great continually asked for news of a Cossack expedition which, under his orders, had been sent out to solve the mystery of a greatly desired "possible isthmus" which he thought must join the continents of Asia and the Americas. An extract from the directions personally addressed by the Tsar to the leaders of this quest shows what degree of pioneering work was expected, even in 1719, of Cossack enterprise.

"You are to proceed to Kamchatka, as you have been ordered, and determine whether Asia and America are united, and go not only North and South, but East and West, putting in a chart all that you see." (See Golder's *"Russian Expansion in the Pacific,"* p. 114, etc.)

If the tossing waters of Behring Strait had not stopped the long ride of the Cossack pioneers, the western coast of North America might have been added to the Tsar's empire before Anglo- Saxon explorers could have gained a foothold there. A Cossack captain was the first white man to set foot upon the coast of Alaska — thus linking the history of our great Eastern neighbor Siberia with our own. And, while Cossack troopers were fighting to hold a great continent for Civilization — as against Bolshevik "frightfulness" and misrule — in the Siberian capital at Omsk the reputed saints-day of Yermak the Discoverer was solemnly recalled by a parade and review of the armies of Free Russia before his statue at the door of the great Cathedral.

BOGDAN HMELNICKY; A COSSACK NATIONAL HERO

THE magic call of free land had slowly re-peopled the devastated steppes of the Ukraine following the withdrawal of the Tartar invasion. Little did the first hardy Cossack pioneers, who built their homesteads in this "smiling wilderness" know or care that by this act they subjected themselves to the feudal claims of former Polish and Lithuanian overlords. Too feeble to make good their pretensions against the Tartars, these nobles now sought to exercise their "rights" over the newcomers. But until the middle of the seventeenth century some acknowledged leader had been lacking among the Cossack chieftains. Until this time the very name of Cossack had indicated a "masterless" man, differentiating their race from the Russian peasant class who had long since bartered liberty in exchange for order. In Bogdan Hmelnicky the scattered settlements and clans of the steppes found a hero through whose genius their warlike race was to receive for a brief period the impulse of nationality.

The industry and courage of the Cossacks had brought prosperity if not peace to the deserted steppes. The Polish aristocrats of the border, *panye* and *starostsi*, were now for the first time safe behind the bulwark of their settlements, and already had begun to look with disfavour on their democratic protectors. Rightly enough, they considered that the *"Free People"* were dangerous neighbors for their own serfs, meek, priest-ridden folk exploited alike by Jew and Jesuit.

In our own day when the problems of a *"Free Poland"* unite the sympathies of the victorious democracies, it is difficult to realize the meaning that *"Polish Freedom"* must have conveyed to the peasant and Cossack population of the Ukraine two centuries ago. The persistent loyalty with which the Polish people have clung to their faith and their nationality has won the admiration of the whole civilized world. Yet the most superficial study of Polish national history reveals the reason for many of their past misfortunes.

The only recognized citizens of the old "republic" of Poland were the *panye*, or nobles, – a class so jealous of its arrogant equality that the negative vote of a single gentleman could set at naught the deliberations of the entire nobiliary body gathered in council. Their parliaments were usually held in the open fields near Cracow or Warsaw, often on horseback. These were attended by all of aristocratic lineage who chose to be present, either to vote or to impose their opinions by their shouts or the clash of their weapons. The great Polish nobles often attended these assemblies accompanied by private armies of horse, foot and artillery, recruited from among their serfs and retainers. Naturally, few of these armed assizes passed off without conflict and the spilling of much azure blood.

No Polish *pan* might engage in trade. To buy and sell was considered degrading and, therefore, forbidden their class. Yet these strange "republican" aristocrats might become the humble servants of a fellow *pan* without losing their rights in the national assembly. Only the nobles were permitted to own land, and too often the exploitation of their peasants was left in the hands of Jew or German "factors" or overseers. The only occupation of the masters of the soil lay in the more congenial employments of law-making – and law-breaking. In the tumultuous assemblies of the nobiliary Diet only one principle seems to have met with general agreement – the God-given right of the *pan* to exploit his serfs as natural "property." Among the free peasants and Cossacks of the Ukraine it was commonly reported that the Polish priests taught their peasant parishioners to answer a question of the-catechism beginning "Why has God created you?" by the humble response: "To give our service to our noble lords."

The civilization of Poland was Catholic and Roman: the civilization of the border provinces looked towards the East and remembered Byzance. These differences have persisted to the present time, but in the early seventeenth century, when Catholic Poland was a powerful state and Russia still in the making, religious oppression sowed the seed of differences which have not yet died away. The people of the Orthodox Ukraine – peasants and Cossacks alike – could only look to a distant Tsar for redress when the armed emissaries of the oppressing Polish Church rode among them demanding tithes and taxes. Or else – as the wise King Sigismond of Poland is reported to have himself advised them – they might "trust to their own Cossack swords."

The complete reunion of Poland and Lithuania decreed at Lublin in 1569 had resulted in a promise to the Greek Orthodox population of the border lands that the freedom of their religion would be respected. But the militant Catholic order of the Society of Jesus was firmly entrenched at Warsaw. To the influence of these learned and courtly prelates the Polish aristocracy owed their astonishing progress in the arts of civilization and their, perhaps too faithful, conformity to the more superficial standards of western Europe. The not unnatural ambition of the Jesuits — and of the Polish nobles whose political policy as well as their conscience was dominated by these spiritual directors, — lay in bringing about the submission of the Orthodox provinces of the Polish frontier to the rule of the Catholic church. By one of those able compromises which formed the basis of Jesuit diplomacy, they conceived the idea of endowing these border races with a separate "Uniate" church. This allowed the Orthodox believers to retain some features of the old ritual, to which they clung so persistently, while yielding obedience to the Pope at Rome. But this first crafty step towards a more irrevocable union was viewed with not unnatural suspicion from the beginning. In 1595 all but thirty-seven of the bishops whose sees lay in the Orthodox provinces had succumbed to the powerful influence of the Jesuits. Not so, however, their parishioners, the sturdy Ukrainian peasantry and the Cossack *polki*. To these latter Orthodoxy meant personal liberty and the dignity of freemen, while Catholicism preached obedience and blind submission.

The lot of the Orthodox clergy and peasants of the Ukraine, separated by a gulf of fanaticism from their feudal Polish lords, was voiced in Morris Drecninski's protest to the King in the Polish Diet:

"When your Majesty goes to war against the Turk who furnishes the greater part of your army? Russians practicing the Orthodox faith! How, then, can we be asked to sacrifice our lives abroad when at home there is no peace? Our miseries, the miseries of the Russian subjects of Poland, are patent to everyone. In the great cities seals close the doors of our churches and their holy treasuries are despoiled. In our monasteries the monks are driven forth and cattle stabled in their place. Our children are without baptism and their corpses are thrown out from the town like the bodies of dead animals. Men and women must live together without God's benediction given by a priest. Death is without confession or sacrament. Is not this an offence against God and will not God avenge us?"

Another grievance, even more galling to the Orthodox frontiersmen, was found in the behaviour of the Jew and German "intendants" who usually acted as intermediaries between the Polish lords of the manor and the long-suffering population of their estates. These "unbelievers" were often given "control of the rights of hunting and fishing, the roads and wine shops" – even access to the Orthodox churches was to be obtained from them only by paying a fee.

The bitterest irony of the situation we have described lay in the fact that these burdens were laid by the aristocracy, not as in the rest of Europe, upon a grovelling population of serfs to whom their lords at least afforded protection, but upon a border nation of alien faith and blood who, following the policy of the Polish kings, possessed a system of martial preparedness and, indeed, were the principal protectors of the Polish frontiers.

The rampart against the Turks and Tartars, formed by the Cossack settlements, had by this time become fully organized. They formed no less than twenty regular Cossack *polki* or regiments, each under its own colonel, or *polkovnik*. The whole of this well disciplined army obeyed the commands of a single military chief called the "Hetman of the Ukraine," who received his appointment from the King of Poland. In all his decisions this officer was guided by the advice of a *starshina* or council of the Cossack elders.

Besides the above troops, recruited from among the inhabitants of the Cossack settlements and the "*slovods*" or armed villages nearer the Tartar frontier, the warlike brotherhood of the Zaporogian Cossacks had now grown into a powerful military organization. Their stronghold – the *sitch* –

formed a permanent camp or rendezvous beyond the rapids of the Dnieper. These warriors – famous in all Europe – represented the perfection, or rather the extreme, of devotion to the principles of free Cossack life. Their celebrated infantry were the only troops capable of withstanding the shock of Polish cavalry, the heavily armed *houzars* or hussars of noble birth, and the less showy, but no less invincible dragoons.

In many places along the border the Cossacks had old-established settlements scattered among the serf-tilled lands belonging to the Polish and Lithuanian nobles. Often these homesteads, which the Cossacks had reclaimed from the steppes, were tenaciously claimed through some shadowy feudal right by absentee Polish landlords. By the latter, the Free Cossacks and their institutions were of course considered a dangerous example to the docile Polish peasantry.

In order to discourage the growth of a class of Cossack proprietors, even the tolerant Polish king, Stephen Bathory, had tried to establish a register of "Free Cossacks" whose numbers were not to exceed six thousand. The surplus of the Cossacks – those not needed for purposes of border defense – were often forced to labor on the land of some feudal lord. It was concerning the coveted right of inscription upon this list of free men and upon grounds of religious oppression that the principal difference now arose which was to separate the Cossack nation from their allegiance to the kings of Poland. Long patient under wrongs, they felt the power to redress: the Cossacks of the Ukraine only awaited a hero to lead them in a war of rightful assertion and protest.

Bogdan Hmelnicky had been chosen by the Swedish King of Poland, Vladislas (or Valdemar) Vasa, as Hetman of the Cossacks of the Ukraine, on account of his record as a soldier, and because judged by the standards of his time, he possessed "no small share of learning" – the ability both to read and write. Such talents were almost a mark of erudition among the Cossacks of the seventeenth century. In his youth a brilliant defense of the fortress of Zolkiev against the Crimean Tartars had made his reputation known even in Europe, where the gazettes were always much concerned with Polish affairs.

The incident which changed Bogdan from a conscientious official of the Polish crown and made him the implacable enemy of his former patrons is recorded in different ways by contemporary historians, – usually according to their race or prejudices. All are agreed that he was the victim of a cruel wrong, and even a Polish writer of his time finds his principal fault to have been that "he revenged himself upon the state for a private iniquity."

Bogdan was a "free-holder" or non-noble proprietor of a small farm and flour mill at a place called Czehrin near the shores of the Dnieper. His little property lay in a country where for leagues around the land was owned, or rather claimed, by the great Polish family of Konietspolski. The intendant of these feudal lords casting a covetous eye on the Naboth's vineyard belonging to the Cossack *hetman*, summoned him before a tribunal pre- sided over by their common 'master, Alexander Konietspolski. Here, after due process of feudal law, Bogdan heard himself summarily dispossessed. To protest against such a sentence was unheard-of insolence. Yet the *hetman* (although he knew that Cossack "rights" stood little chance of prevailing against a Polish magnate who himself interpreted the laws) ventured to take this step – trusting in his record of past services to the "republic." As an all-sufficient answer, the veteran soldier was sentenced to serve a term in the jail of the Konietspolski.

Fortunately for the Cossack nation, Bogdan was able to make his escape, and we soon find him an honoured guest in that citadel of personal liberty, the impenetrable *sitch* of the Zaporogians. Among the island fortresses defended by this famous brotherhood, even the armed retainers of Konietspolski dared not pursue him. Meanwhile, the intendant, Czaplinski, in order to revenge himself in true seignorial fashion, visited Bogdan's homestead at the head of his retainers. The crime that ensued is recounted in many ways. The poetical necessities of the case may have caused the Cossack ballad- historians to rouse their countrymen by painting the intendant's conduct in its blackest colours. Czaplinski, besides depriving the *hetman* of his property sought, in his absence, "to place upon the honour of his victim's family an unspeakable outrage."

The whole incident is but one in a long story of oppression, yet it was the spark necessary to fire the powder magazine of Cossack indignation and to rouse their fierce resistance to wrongs they had too long patiently endured. The war which now began between the nobles of the Polish "republic" on the one hand and the Free Cossacks and Ukrainian peasants on the other was to end only after the fairest provinces of the border land had again and again been devastated with "fire and sword."

It was at the head of nearly 100,000 Cossack soldiers and a horde of Tartars whom the promised plunder of the Polish castles had enlisted on the side of their bitterest enemies, that the *hetman* returned to demand an accounting from the Konietpolski. As he advanced, new volunteers flocked to his standards: Cossacks, peasants, and gentlemen of the Ukraine, whom religious persecution had driven from their estates. In the space of a few weeks he found himself the leader of an army of irregular troops estimated at 300,000 men — a whole people in arms. From now on until his death Bogdan was an uncrowned king — the head of a Cossack nation for the first time united. As a symbol or scepter of authority he carried in his hand a reed from the shores of the River Dneiper.

Thinking to crush without difficulty this motley gathering (for in spite of the stiffening battalions of Zaporogian frontiersmen the Cossack *polki* were scarcely a match for the regular troops maintained by the Polish republic) a brilliant company of nobles set forth from Warsaw "as to the chase." Their leader was a brave young general – Stephen Pototski. At Zoltivody – the Yellow Waters – this army of Polish nobles thought to ride roughshod over the peasant bands, but their own defeat was complete and crushing.

Vladislas, the King of Poland – the wise ruler of a distracted nobility – received on his deathbed a message from Bogdan. Although the Cossack-chieftain was now victorious, his letter was a submissive proposal (dated June 2, 1648) suggesting, not dictating, the terms of an honourable peace. The principal privilege asked for was an assurance that the "ancient rights" of the Cossacks, notably the famous "Register of Freemen," should be restored, and that the right of free worship be allowed to those of the Greek-Orthodox faith. Perhaps the very mildness of the tone of Bogdan's communication deceived Prince Jeremy Visnowiecki, the new chief of the Polish armies. Prince Jeremy was the embodiment of Jesuitical intolerance and well-born arrogance, but to these defects he joined one doubtful virtue – stupid and uncalculating courage. Strengthened by a few minor successes among his own revolted villages, he now thought only of punishing the offenders. "Strike so that they may feel!!" he had ordered his judges and executioners. The story of his "frightfulness" brought to the Cossack camp new and more desperate levies of volunteers.

No reply had even been vouchsafed by the proud nobility to Bogdan's proposal of peace. Indeed none was awaited: on foreign agent and Jesuit priest — the twin scourges of the long-suffering Orthodox peasants of the Ukraine — fell the weight of Cossack vengeance. The stories of the wrongs of these "martyrs" have generally survived the grievances they provoked. It is but fair, however, to search for some underlying motive of justice behind the Cossack brutalities which have been so eloquently exploited. In spite of the naturally prejudiced accounts of Polish historians, the student of the present day will find something besides blind ferocity in the acts of this "coalition of Mussulmen, Socinians and Greeks," who in their furious crusade overthrew churches, burned monasteries, "granting their lives to monks and nuns only to enjoy the spectacle of their forced nuptials, celebrated in the shadow of the sword."

Fleeing before the advancing Cossack army, a horde of fugitives: old men, women and children, the inhabitants of the border villages, brought to the castles and cities of Poland the first news of these unexpected, unbelievable disasters to her armies. Thus at a time when Western Europe was celebrating the end of thirty years of continual bloodshed by signing the treaty of Westphalia, the border world of the Slav nation took up the burden of war.

After the death of the wise Vladislas, a great Plenary Diet of the nobles of Poland was held on the field of Volna. While the excitable *Panye* screamed recriminations at each other's heads — trying in disorderly conclave to elect a new king for their distracted nation — Jeremy Visnowiecki with an army of 140,000 men, nobles of Poland with their serfs and mercenaries, tried to stem the tide of invasion at Plavace. But at the approach of the Cossacks and their allies this forlorn hope, gathered from all her wide lands to meet Poland's extremity, melted away in most ungentlemanly panic before the waving of Bogdan's reed — the peasant standard.

Bogdan's wise policy now spared the farmsteads and the Roman Catholic churches dear to the Polish peasants. But upon the castles of the nobility, stored with treasures of art which excited the admiration of every European traveller who had visited these distant lands, the advancing host wreaked its anger. Bogdan no longer desired a mere Cossack vengeance. He was now the leader of a popular movement or *jacquerie* which sought to secure the same privilege for the peasants of Poland that his victories promised for the Cossack inhabitants of the Ukraine. While the only electors of the "republic" – the privileged nobles – still deliberated at Volna over the choice of a king, Bogdan had become the undisputed ruler of the Ukraine. By establishing popular rule over an ever increasing expanse of Polish territory, he seemed about to solve the problem of who should be king, in his own way.

In the castle at Zamosc, one of the last of the "impregnable" fortresses of the Polish borders, the armies of Bogdan were besieging a distinguished company including the heads of nearly all the greatest feudal families of the western provinces. Here, with their servants and treasures, were gathered the refugees of Plavace, the lords and ladies of the great families of Viesnowiecki, Zamoyski, Sobieski, besides others of lesser note. To join in the defense of this last stronghold of his caste, John Sobieski, the future hero of all Christian Europe, had passed during the night through the triple lines of the Cossack armies.

Under this brilliant young chieftain the besieged forces still held out, when after five weeks of armed debate the choice of the electors of Poland fell at last upon the candidate least obnoxious to the majority of the electors. The honour was thrust upon an unwilling prelate, the Cardinal

John Cazimir, a brother of the late king. This solution appeared preferable to a choice of the Russian Tsar Alexis, whose ambitious plans would have joined Poland and Russia in a "personal union."

Cardinal John Cazimir (who was so strangely to end his days in exile as Abbot of the Convent of St. Germain des Prés in Paris) has been described as "too passionate for the Church, too feeble for the throne and, above all, too honest and straightforward for his time and country." His first royal act showed the latter traits. Refusing to listen to the partisans of Prince Jeremy – who, in spite of the thorough beating the Polish nobles had received, continued to threaten the rebellious Cossacks with all manner of legal punishments solemnly voted in high conclave of the Diet – he offered to treat with Bogdan's armies on the basis of their old guarantees.

Over his royal signature, he wrote to their leader, proposing almost in the terms used between sovereign and sovereign, that the past be forgotten. At the same time he promised to revive and confirm the ancient privileges of the Cossacks which had been so treacherously violated by the Jeremites. The royal messenger was instructed to deliver at the same time to Bogdan, if he were prepared to accept them, the horse-tail standard and other regalia formerly conferred on every Cossack *hetman* by the kings of Poland. Although the fortunes of war had raised the man thus honoured above the power of the Polish throne, Bogdan placed his lips respectfully upon the King's signature. As a proof of immediate obedience, he ordered that the final assault about to be delivered upon the castle of Zamosc should be abandoned. Chivalrously trusting to the royal word, the army of Cossacks and peasants was removed some ten miles from the walls of this last battered stronghold of Polish nobility. But the generosity of the Cossack chieftain and the hopes of the popular party were once more to be deceived. By breaking the royal promises, Prince Jeremy and a band of confederated "nobles" were able to throw themselves upon the undefended camp of the Cossacks, winning a treacherous but temporary advantage. The unfortunate Cazimir, although a stranger to the acts of Jeremy and protesting against such violation of his agreement, was none the less forced to march to the assistance of the Polish forces.

Still wearing the rich garments they had donned in honour of the Cardinal's marriage with his brother's widow, the Polish court set forth to attack the indefatigable Bogdan. But by the time they had reached the frontier, this amazing wedding cortège (whose warlike pomp astonished even the accompanying envoys from the great courts of Europe) learned of a second well-deserved defeat of the perjured "Jeremites." Their own peril now became imminent. At Zborovo the embroidered tents and silken pavilions of the royal army were soon surrounded and beset by the Cossack and peasant troops. Only the sudden defection of their undependable ally, the Khan of Crimea, saved Cazimir and his bride. The Khan had been won over to the Polish side by the promised renewal of the degrading Polish tribute paid his ancestors. In view of this temporary respite the angry Bogdan once more consented to negotiate.

The old terms of the Cossack demands were magnanimously renewed. The popular party chiefly insisted upon the expulsion of both Jews and Jesuits from the Orthodox provinces. The rights of the metropolitan of Kiev to a seat in the Senate of Warsaw and the opening of the Cossack registers to enroll 40,000 Cossacks – who were thus protected from the claims and exploitation of the Polish landholders – was also secured. In a final clause Bogdan was recognized by the King of Poland as his deputy and *hetman* over all the provinces of Little Russia, thus securing the practical autonomy of the Ukraine provinces.

After the peace of Zborovo, Bogdan had written to the Polish king as follows: — "Through his own example, my father taught me loyalty in my cradle by dying for the republic. If I have been forced to spill noble blood, whose is the fault? Let your Majesty inquire of the nobles who surround him I I am ready, Sire, to satisfy all your Majesty's desires and, for my own part, no false pride shall interfere. I only ask one thing: the certainty of living in peace under Your Majesty's laws." The unfortunate John Cazimir, Bodgan recognized as a statesman in whose word he could trust. But the Polish nobility of that day could not feel their "honour" involved in keeping faith with such low-born enemies. The years that followed, marking alas! but a truce in the popular strife, were fatal chapters in the national story of Poland. It is impossible to find any true record of this time. The only historical sources are so filled with the recriminations and exaggerations of their authors as to be almost useless to the student.

Over the whole Ukraine hangs a red mist, the firelit smoke rising from hamlet and château. Hidden by this pall the forms of the contestants are but dimly seen: peasant mobs, wild Cossack troops, and the brilliantly armed retainers of the *panye* of the Polish "republic." Above the charge and shock of the contending armies rise the woeful cries of thousands of innocent victims sacrificed by this horrible civil carnage. Even the heroic Bogdan felt the call of ambition and personal spite. Turning from his pursuit of the national enemy, the *hetman* of the Ukraine undertook a campaign against Moldavia in order to force the *volovoda* of that province to bestow the hand of his daughter, Rosanda (promised to his personal foe, Jeremy Viesnowiecki), on his own son, Timothy Hmelnicky.

Under the liberal-minded Sultan Mahomed IV. (1650) Constantinople had become a refuge for all the religious exiles of Europe, fleeing from the persecution of their fellow Christians. The Orthodox patriarch in the

Turkish capital induced Bogdan to accept from the Sultan the high title of "Prince of the Ukraine." A little later, the same influences found no difficulty in launching the Cossacks upon a renewed crusade against the Catholics and Jesuitized Uniates of the border provinces.

But the Poles had profited by the respite given them during Bogdan's southern campaigns to strengthen their armies with troops of German mercenaries, whose trade of war had languished in Eastern Europe since the Peace of Westphalia. Bogdan and his Cossacks, encamped near Zboraz, ravaging at their leisure the lands of the Viesnowiecki, found himself attacked by these formidable reinforcements. Although the Cossacks defended themselves courageously behind their famous "tabors" — ramparts formed by ox-carts — the fortunes of the day remained with the professional soldiery of Tilly and Wallenstein. Moreover, the promised Turkish reinforcements failed to arrive in aid of Bogdan at the critical moment.

After the temporary advantages thus gained by the party of the nobles the famous Cossack Register was reduced to 20,000. But rather than return to the fields of their Polish oppressors, great numbers of Cossacks emigrated to join their brethren on Russian territory. In the *stanitzi* on the shores of the Don and Volga, they were more free to exercise their national customs at the same time the Tsar's armies were strengthened by recruits ever ready for a new attack upon the Polish frontier. Bogdan had, moreover, fully realized that the pride of the Polish nobles could learn nothing by experience. Their determination to exercise ruthlessly their "rights" over the peasants who had entrusted their fortunes to the Cossack alliance was shown by every new act of the Diet. With a nation controlled only by class feeling, no compromise can be made, no agreements held. Already their fellows were deserting the Cossack settlements in alarming numbers to place themselves under the protection of the Tsar on Russian territory. The time had come for Bogdan and the Cossacks of the Dnieper to make their choice.

About this time an ambassador of the Tsar, Prince Buturline, visited the Cossack camp, and Bogdan assembled the chiefs of the Cossack nation to consult with this official. At Perieslav, their assembly was asked to decide the future of the Ukraine nation. The *hetman* began his speech as follows: –

"My lord colonels, scribes and captains: and you, noble army of the Zaporogians: All of you, christians of the Orthodox faith, are witnesses that we can no longer live, except under the protection of a prince. We have a choice of four masters: The Sultan of Turkey, the King of Poland, the Khan of the Crimea, or the Tsar." Continuing his long harangue, he pointed out many reasons (notably their common religion) that caused him to give his own vote in favor of a Russian alliance. A loud shout of assent greeted his words. It was decided to send a deputation without delay to the Tsar Alexis, beseeching him to take his "children of Little Russia" under his protection. In an assembly of the Russian States General summoned by Alexis, the strong argument was advanced that unless the offers of Bogdan were accepted, the whole Cossack nation might be forced to place itself under the protection of Turkey or the "Crim Tartars." Reasons of policy decided the Russians to incorporate these turbulent new citizens within the empire, but it is to be noted that no other "conquest" of the Ukraine ever took place.

Meanwhile, Timothy Hmelnicky had once more set out to seek his fatal bride, Rosanda. Attacked by the Poles on the banks of the river Bug, he defeated them with great slaughter. While the interrupted nuptials of Bogdan's son and heir with Jeremy's betrothed were celebrated, the Polish

Diet in the extremity of its despair begged for military aid from the Diet of the empire at Ratisbon.

At the present time, the reasons offered as an excuse for such an appeal are worthy of note: "Fighting always in the name of liberty this slogan strengthens the Cossack's cause. If left to themselves the Cossacks may even find partisans in Silesia ready to help them. For these reasons the Emperor's help is implored." Failing to move the Emperor, the Diet next addressed itself to the Khan of the Crimea, although one of their principal grievances against Bogdan had been the Cossack alliance with the Tartars. This ferocious ally, whose help they could only hope to secure on condition that two of their Polish provinces be given to his troops for pillage, also refused his support.

Although distrusting the Polish nobles, with whom he was but nominally at peace, and in spite of the successes of the Cossack party, the Tsar Alexis still hesitated in his decision. Bogdan, whose son Timothy had fallen in a border skirmish, now renewed his demands that the Russians should accept the Cossack alliance. According to Salvandy the final argument which decided the Tsar to make war with Poland was the victory of a bull named "Moscovy" over another named "Poland," during one of those trials by "ordeal" in which the credulity of that day still saw the judgment of a higher power. The mathematical academy of Warsaw (a fact authenticated by a despatch of the Emperor's envoy) was at the same time engaged in a profound astrological calculation, whose results bore out the judgment of Alexis' bulls, but in a sense, of course, favourable to their own country.

The final excuse for opening hostilities by a Russian advance against the Polish provinces was found in the studied arrogance of the Polish diplomats, who, in spite of the continued remonstrances of Alexis' envoys, insisted upon addressing the Tsar with one "*etc.*" less than the majesty of his imperial titles required.

The Moscovite armies quickly overran Lithuania, capturing in succession Vilna, Grodno and Kovno, long centres of contention between the armies of Russia and Poland. Meanwhile Bogdan and his Cossacks advanced upon the border provinces of the south, capturing the proud city of Lemberg, whose burghers enjoyed the rights of Polish nobility. Few writers of the time seem to have realized that the whole political balance of Eastern Europe was about to change. A new "Great Empire" whose weight in the future councils of Europe was to become preponderant, had come into existence. The defection of the Cossacks from their Polish alliance turned the scales of the balanced forces at the command of the two great Slav states in favour of Russia. Henceforth Poland was to remain on the defensive in all her struggles with her mighty neigbbour.

By a strange turn of events, now briefly to be described in their relation to the Cossack cause, the appearance of a third enemy in the field alone saved the Polish state. Charles X of Sweden, alarmed by the rapid success of the Russians in Lithuania, tried to secure a share of the spoil for Sweden. After conquering – with the help of Polish malcontents – the great cities of Posen, Warsaw and Cracow, he allowed himself to be elected King of Poland by the distracted Diet. With little love for the "republic" of which he was now the titular head, he turned his armies and ambitions against the Tsar in her defense. The Polish nation, trampled underfoot by this double conquest, could henceforth only profit by the quarrels of its destroyers over their spoils, to preserve for more than a century a precarious independence.

In judging of Bogdan's conduct in connection with the complicated situation which now arose, it must be remembered that the freedom and privileges of the Cossack nation in the Ukraine had been the primary object of his momentous revolt against Poland. He had indeed appeared to abandon this ambition for independence by placing the Cossack nation under the rule of the Tsar Alexis. Although the Assembly of Perieslav and the decisions taken under Bogdan's influence became the most significant and lasting event of his career, the situation created by the invasion of the Swedes caused him to regret this alliance with Russia. Once more the Cossacks dreamed of a third great Slav state, which their valor might establish in the "land of Rus." In the later plans of Bogdan we may perhaps find the first signs of the Rutheno-Slav or Ukrainian movement of the present day.

In January 1657, the Voievoda of Transylvania, George Rakovsky, invaded the distracted Polish "republic" as the ally of Charles of Sweden. A dismemberment of Poland now threatened, which might have anticipated the events which occurred more than a century later. Bogdan and his Cossacks saw in the onslaughts of this newcomer an opportunity to recover the liberties which had been lost or restricted by their agreements with the Tsar. Although joining their forces to the new enemy of their Polish oppressors, the Cossacks found themselves allied to an avowed enemy of Russia. The maritime nations of Europe now began to take part in these complicated struggles of the Northern Powers. The jealous intervention of Sweden's old enemies, the rival sea-powers of Denmark and Holland, forced Charles to retire from Poland in such haste that in his retreat, he had not even time to notify his allies. Rakovsky escaped the anger of the Poles through a series of humiliating concessions, only to fall into the hands of the Tartars while retreating homewards. Thus, in the short space of six weeks, through a series of unforeseen events and combinations which their own courage did little to bring about, the Polish nobles found their territory rid of the devastating presence of three armies.

At this embarrassing juncture in the affairs of the Cossacks – hated by the Poles and separated from their Russian allies – there disappeared from the scene a man, who, in the turmoil of these events had played so great and singular a part. "Able, both as a statesman and a warrior, accorded a kingly state by all the Great Powers, Bogdan continued until the end of his career to lead the life of a peasant or a common soldier. In the same room that he shared with his wife and children he received embassies from the greatest crowned heads of Europe. The sudden apoplectic stroke which carried off the veteran chief of the Cossacks removed a factor which, for ten years, had played a rôle in Eastern Europe which has been compared to that of Cromwell in the West. Yet today Bogdan's name is all but forgotten in history.

While readers of the English race may consider exaggerated a parallel between the Cossack Bogdan and the great Protector, we must take into account in our judgment of these men and their ambitions, the widely different circumstances which confronted them. Both tried, in the name of liberty, to build into free states nations just emerging from the tyranny of feudal institutions. Both sought to maintain independent of the autocratic governments that surrounded them, democracies anticipating those of our own day.

But, by "freedom" it is to be feared the Cossack comrades of Bogdan understood little except license. During the siege of Zamosc at the most fatal moment of their national fortunes, even the prestige of Bogdan's leadership could not prevent large numbers of his followers from deserting the Cossack camp in order to place in safety the rich spoils of the chaâteaux pillaged by the way. The Cossack troopers that remained, "astonished to find themselves eating their coarse rations from silver plates, drinking from golden goblets and sleeping on couches covered with the richest furs, passed their days and nights in orgies and masquerades. Simple peasants, dressed in the stolen trappings of noble bishops and palatines wasted the stern opportunities their courage had won."

With the death of Bogdan the free Cossack state he had founded in the Ukraine fell to pieces almost in a night – nor were his great projects revived until recent times.

THE STRUGGLE FOR THE UKRAINE

BOGDAN left to his surviving son a splendid heritage – the duty of carrying out great projects but half realized. Soon after his father's death George Hmelnicky found even his right to the hetmanship contested by John Wykowski, a Cossack representing the faction favorable to Poland. The young hetman threw himself upon the mercies of the Tsar Alexis, but the majority of the Cossack settlements once more temporarily united themselves with Poland, lured by the promise, readily broken, that they should enjoy nationality as an independent duchy under the Polish crown.

The Cossack officers of this faction now began to copy the manners of the Polish *panye* fatuously dreaming of a nobility of their own. At Knotop the Hetman Wykowski led these "free" Cossacks for the last time to victory against the Russian troops. But factions known as the parties of the "Left and Right Bank" (i. e. of the river Dnieper, forming the geographical boundary between the two Slav nations) divided the Cossacks who still professed allegiance to Poland into two opposing parties. Moreover the Polish nobles, blinded by their fanatical faith in their feudal rights, lost every opportunity of rallying the Cossacks to their standard. Religious intolerance soon played its fatal rôle. The Catholic bishop of Cracow grossly insulted the Orthodox metropolitan of Kiev, whose place had been assured him in the Plenary Council of the Diet. The Greek-Orthodox Cossacks, maddened by this act, joined in a sudden massacre of the adherents of the Hetman Wykowski. Under the leadership of the son of Bogdan the majority of the Cossack settlements returned once more to their Russian allegiance. The fairest provinces of the ancient "land of Rus," Kiev, Poltava and the broad steppes of the Ukraine were lost forever to the Polish Crown. Even in their undeveloped state these rich borderlands were recognized both by the rulers of Russia and Poland to be a prize essential to the predominance of their states.

A vivid description of the appearance of the Ukraine at this time is to be found in Sienkiewicz famous work, *"With Fire and Sword."*

"The last traces of settled life ended on the way to the south, at no great distance beyond Chigirin on the side of the Dnieper, and on the side of the Dniester not far from Uman; thence forward to the bays and sea there was nothing but steppe after steppe, hemmed in by the two rivers as by a frame. At the bend of the Dnieper in the lower country beyond the cataracts Cossack life was seething, but in the open plains no man dwelt; only along the shores were nestled here and there little fields, like islands in the sea. The land belonged in name to Poland, but it was an empty land, in which the Commonwealth permitted the Tartars to graze their herds; but since the Cossacks prevented this frequently, the field of pasture was a field of battle too.

How many struggles were fought in that region, how many people had laid down their lives there, no man had counted, no man remembered. Eagles, falcons, and ravens alone saw these; and whoever from a distance was heard the sound of wings and the call of ravens, whoever beheld the whirl of birds circling over one place, knew that corpses or unburied bones were lying beneath. Men were hunted in the grass as wolves or wild goats. All who wished engaged in this hunt. Fugitives from the law defended themselves in the wild steppes. The armed herdsman guarded his flock, the warrior sought adventure, the robber plunder, the Cossack a Tartar, the Tartar a Cossack. It happened that whole bands guarded herds from troops of robbers. The steppe was both empty and filled, quiet and terrible, peaceable and full of ambushes; wild by reason of its wild plains, but wild, too, from the wild spirit of men.

At times a great war filled it. Then there flowed over it like waves Tartar *chambuls*, Cossack regiments, Polish or Wallachian companies. In the night-time the neighing of horses answered the howling of wolves, the voices of drums and brazen trumpets flew on to the island of Ovid and the sea, and along the black trail of Kutchman there seemed an inundation of men. The boundaries of the Commonwealth were guarded from Kamenyets to the Dnieper by outposts and *stanitzi*; and when the roads were about to swarm with people, it was known especially by the countless flocks of birds which, frightened by the Tartars, flew onward to the north. But the Tartar, if he slipped out from the Black Forest or crossed the Dniester from the Wallachian side, came by the southern provinces together with the birds."

*

By the terms of the Treaty of Andrusov, signed January 13th, 1667, the Tsar and the King of Poland came to a first definite arrangement covering the territories of Ukraine. This document carefully defined the influence each monarch was to exercise upon the Cossack settlements of the Dnieper. The classic stream became effectively the boundary between the two states. Kiev, the capital of Little Russia, was left (pending future negotiations, to which the Tsar Alexis looked forward without anxiety) in the hands of the Russians. The administration of the turbulent Zaporogian sitch was made subject to the joint "protection" of both Crowns, a pretension which, needless to say, the "Republic of the Free Cossacks beyond the Cataracts" disclaimed with scorn. Both high contracting parties agreed not to enlist in their respective armies subjects of the other crown, nor to encourage the emigration from one bank to another of Cossacks settled in their respective territory.

A final article of the treaty solemnly set forth that neither King nor Tsar should interfere with any measures which the other High Contracting Party should deem necessary in order to discipline these new, involuntary subjects. At first kept secret, the clauses of this treaty which thus disposed of their territory without their consent became known to the Cossacks on both sides of the river. The settlements blazed with indignation. Doroshenko the *hetman* elected by the Polish faction, and Brukowicki, the *hetman* appointed by the Tsar, became equally objects of suspicion among the men of their own parties. A tumultuous invasion was immediately made by the Zaporogians upon the neigbbouring Polish and Russian provinces in the defense of the "National Liberties." Every party now understood the term "Freedom" to mean the right to sack and pillage unrestrained the fair territory of the Ukraine whose interest all professed to defend. These disorders finally resulted in a second convention with Russia, to which the majority of the Cossacks adhered.

Under the Hetman Samoilovitch devoted to the cause of the Tsar, the imperial power was greatly extended. By the signature of a new peace at Moscow in 1686 both Kiev and Smolensk were abandoned by Poland to the administration of Russia, the Tsar undertaking to maintain order along the troubled frontiers of the Crimean Tartars, thus leaving Sobieski free to continue his famous crusade against his sworn enemy, the Turkish Sultan.

Through the skilful diplomacy of the Tsar Alexis — even greater as an empire builder than his son Peter the Great — these negotiations finally resulted in drawing closer the bond uniting the Cossack class to the Russian Crown. Their obstinate pride and determination to exercise their feudal "rights" over a free and warlike population had lost to the Polish nobles of the frontier the jurisdiction they had formerly claimed. It must not be supposed, however, that in passing to Russian allegiance the Cossacks abandoned their claim to autonomy.

The story of the Cossack revolts during the eighteenth century fills an important page in Russian history.

*

Even under the régime of the last Romanovs a service was held every year in many of the churches of Russia for the solemn cursing — with full ritual — of all religious and political heretics who in the past had ventured to disturb the public order of the empire. Mentioned separately the names of "the False Dmitri," Boris Godounov, Stenka Razin, Mazeppa and Pougatchev were greeted by the clergy with thundering responses of "Anathema! Anathema!"

The fact that three of the persons judged worthy of this curious distinction were Cossacks, while "the False Dmitri" generally enjoyed their support, would seem to demonstrate that even the potent brew contained in the "melting-pot" of Russian imperialism found difficulty in absorbing such recalcitrant elements as the "Republics" of the Dnieper, the Don and the Jaik.

In spite of its brief importance, the Cossack revolt led by Stenka Razin in the years 1671-3 may be dismissed as an outbreak of border ruffianism led by a particularly successful river pirate and brigand. Profiting by a time of famine and distress along the Volga, Razin became a kind of border Robin Hood, enjoying the popularity easily acquired by anyone who pretends to revenge the wrongs of the poor upon the purses of the rich. His name will, moreover, always be remembered in Russia for its connection with the unforgetable lilt of the song "Volga, Volga," etc. But his overthrow near Zimbirsk by Bariatinski and his execution at Moscow put a sudden end to a career which left no aftermath. The early years of the reign of Peter I were troubled by a series of revolts or mutinies in the Cossack territories of the Don, which, although ending in a severe punishment of the ringleaders, exhibited the determination of this important branch of the "Free People" not to allow their privileges to be overridden by the growing power of the autocracy.

As in the previous two centuries, the flight or emigration of their serfs from the estates of the *boyars* in the north had continued to excite the apprehension of the Russian nobles. During the opening years of the *eighteenth* century it was calculated that the call of liberty and free land had drawn nearly 30,000 serfs to the Cossack settlements of the Don. The Tsar, Peter the Great, whose far-reaching reforms did not contemplate any immediate amelioration of the lot of the peasants or the conditions of serfdom, now determined to send Prince Dolgorouki to force these fugitives to return. While the Cossacks of the Don at first formally submitted to the authority of the Tsar's envoy, they privately determined in solemn council to support the new companions who had thus loyally sought their protection. Dolgorouki at first met with little opposition. During his return journey, however, while encumbered with troops of captives, he was led into a Cossack ambush where the peasants were released and his army all but destroyed. The fact that a leader in this assault, a Cossack named Boulavin, was subsequently elected *hetman*, added a fresh provocation to the previous conduct of the Don Cossacks.

The result of these events was not long awaited. Peter, realizing that any weakness he might show in meeting the situation might end in a general revolt of the provinces of the Ukraine, sent another Prince Dolgorouki with fresh troops to revenge his kinsman upon the inhabitants of the "turbulent provinces of the Don."

"The principal mutineers," wrote this officer a few months later in a grim report addressed to the Emperor, "have been hanged. Of their companions one in every ten have been hanged; all of those I have had hanged were placed upon gibbets, which I erected on the rafts and set afloat, so that along the whole course of the river they might serve as an example."

After the sanguinary hint offered to the Cossacks of the Don, the Tsar was able to introduce his favourite methods of military administration among the "settlements" or *slovods* of the Don without further armed resistance. But the discontent aroused by these innovations was deep and implacable.

In considering the "treason" of Mazeppa and the course adopted by his fellow conspirators during the important events about to be narrated, the unpopularity of these reforms, which infringed some of the most cherished privileges assured by the Tsar's predecessors to the population of the Ukraine, must first be taken into account.

The historians of this period have generally been too deeply in sympathy with the reforming policies of Peter the Great to do full justice to the Cossack cause. The actions of Mazeppa and his Cossack followers are only accounted perfidious obstacles in the pathway of Russia's progress towards unification. There is nothing, however, in the history of this fateful struggle, wherein the defeat of a couple of mutinous regiments of Cossacks and a few thousand exhausted Swedish veterans actually decided the balance of power in the north – to show that Mazeppa acted otherwise than as a disinterested upholder of the rights and national privileges of his adopted comrades in arms.

Consideration of the part played by the Cossacks in the winter campaign of Poltava, throws an important light on the military history of Charles XII. Even the "Madman of the North," in spite of his over-confident (not to say vainglorious) methods of strategy, would never have permitted his army to be drawn so far from its base of supplies unless the assurance of Mazeppa had led him to suppose that a discontented *"Free Ukraine"* party were ready to welcome him as a deliverer.

MAZEPPA

TO have held for an instant the balance of power in the momentous struggle which fixed the supremacy of Russia among the "Powers of the North"; to lose by narrowest chance a great place in history; to be remembered only as the hero of a romantic poem; the central figure of a popular opera, – such has been the strange fate of the Cossack *hetman* Mazeppa!

So complete was the downfall of the great Imperial State which Sweden had planned to encircle the Baltic that Charles XII, whom Voltaire calls the leading military genius of his time, now appears but a pale and legendary figure when contrasted with Peter the Great – the mighty rival over whom he so nearly triumphed. No struggle of the eighteenth Century led to more portentous consequences than the winter campaign ending in the battle of Poltava.

It is significant in view of present events to consider the part played by the Cossacks of the Ukraine during these decisive moments in the world's history. Had the united strength of the Free Cossacks and the Ukrainian peasant-proprietors been exercised on behalf of Charles XII rather than in favor of their oppressor the Tsar, there is little cause to doubt that a great

Ukrainian state might have arisen on the steppes of South Russia, to which the less favored lands of "Great Russia" and the forest regions to the north would perhaps have become tributary. For in spite of their relatively small numbers the warlike caste of the Cossacks possessed not only military training and initiative but also a strong sense of loyalty and fellowship in arms lacking to a great extent among the *moujiki* comprising Peter's armies. Had Mazeppa in addition his military qualities been born a Cossack instead of belonging to the hated Polish race, he might have united his adopted people at this critical moment of their career to face Peter's German-led and German-drilled troops. Napoleon's dictum that Russia is destined to become either Cossack or German appears all the more plausible in the light of the events surrounding the invasion of Charles XII. Indeed the French emperor – a close student and – an ardent admirer of "the Mad King's" strategy – may have based his statement upon his appreciation of the all but forgotten yet fateful events which we shall now briefly review.

Contemporary historians (including Voltaire, who, however, in matters of history scarcely exhibits the same critical spirit that won him so great a reputation in his discussion of religious questions) agree in repeating the romantic episode which transformed the youthful, Mazeppa from a page at the brilliant Polish court into a leader of the rough Cossack bands of the Ukraine.

Their accounts are, in the main, identical with the circumstances narrated in Byron's famous poem. Mazeppa was by birth a Polish noble from the province of Podolia. Through the graces of his person and an education which – at least by comparison – distinguished him among his fellows, he obtained the position of "serving gentleman" in the household of a rich Polish nobleman. The young wife of this notable, having somewhat over frankly exhibited her admiration for Mazeppa's qualities the outraged husband conceived the vengeance which effectually removed Mazeppa from the neighborhood of his inamorata, but with results far different from those planned or expected. The handsome page, bound, naked and defenceless, on the back of an unbroken stallion, instead of succumbing to the roving wolves of the steppes, was carried by his mount among a herd of horses belonging to a camp of wandering Cossacks. Joining this wild company the youth soon found himself enrolled a member of the band, and in the course of a few months his education and personal bravery gave him the post of aide-de-camp to the *hetman*.

At this point the legends surrounding Mazeppa's advent among the Cossacks give place to more authentic accounts. A few years later we find him – risen in turn to the post of *hetman* – carrying on a series of forays in conjunction with Russian troops against the Tartars of the Crimea. These skirmishes resulted in establishing his reputation, not only as a brilliant and successful leader in border warfare, but also as a dependable instrument of Russian policy.

During the first siege of Azof, Peter the Great first learned from personal observation to appreciate the qualities and military capabilities of his new Cossack subjects. When a serious check to the Russian forces occurred before that strong fortress in 1695, it was the mobility and resource of the Cossack levies under Mazeppa that covered the retreat of the famous *"New Armies"* organized by the Tsar on the European model. The Emperor or *"Bombardier Peter,"* serving at the time in their ranks under the command of General Lefort, took part in all the hardships of this retreat. It was, however, through such defeats that every military advantage of Peter the Great was to be obtained. The faulty strategy which had failed to secure his object during these first operations was cast aside and Peter now conceived the idea of capturing Azof by a combined sea and land attack.

On the upper reaches of the river Don, the Tsar began at once to construct his armada, consisting of "twenty-two galleys, a hundred rafts and canoes" The number of the latter craft indicates that the part played by the Cossacks and notably the Zaporogians in these first Russian naval operations must have been a considerable one. Relying on their skill as river boatmen and the tactics developed during many a raid against the Turks in the Black Sea, they were now launched in a sudden attack on the Turkish fleet. Less than 1500 Cossacks manning long river-boats, similar to those used by the Zaporogians, did not hesitate to attack the great Turkish galleys defending the communications by means of which the beleaguered fortress received its provisions from the Turkish colonies of Anatolia.

We can readily imagine with what enthusiasm and anxiety the Tsar followed the fortunes of the Cossack attack. Peter was himself in command of a small wooden frigate. He had now become "Steerman Peter Alexievitch," serving under the command of "Admiral" Lefort (for, together with the principal officers of his staff he had assumed naval titles and duties). Prodigies of valour were displayed in the hand to hand conflict which ensued. Little by little the surprising manœuvres of the handy Cossack flotilla completely overcame the more regular naval strategy of the Turkish commander. The Ottoman fleet was gradually dispersed and the heavy galleys – separated from their fellows and rendered helpless – were captured one by one. This wholly unexpected disaster cut off the Turks from their base of supplies and gave the garrison within the town no other alternative but to raise their turbans on the points of long lances in sign of surrender.

Fifteen hundred ducats were accepted (not, we are told without much grumbling) by the Cossacks instead of the promised right of sacking the town. Mazeppa and his Cossack boatmen were personally thanked by the Tsar — the latter in high good humor because be had himself been promoted to a superior grade by Lefort for the part he had played in the fight. It was thus as actual comrades in arms that the basis of the long friendship between the Emperor and Mazeppa was formed.

In 1705 Peter carried out his wholesale execution of the *streltzi* — the privileged but undependable militia of the old Russian court — a terrible requital for their disloyal behaviour during his famous European tour. Following this event the Cossacks became a more important factor than ever in the border armies of Russia. At the same time, they received as recruits a great number of *streltzi* fleeing from Peter's drastic military reforms. This new element was in all probability largely responsible for the revolt that spread among the Don Cossacks in the following year (1706).

The victories of Azof and the conquest of the shores of the Black Sea awakened the military ambitions of Tsar Peter. Moreover it was at this juncture that the King of Sweden died and his son Charles, a lad but 18 years of age, came to the throne. In the accession of so youthful a prince both the Tsar and the King of Poland saw an opportunity of ridding themselves of a rival power whose ambition, clashed with their own. The position occupied by Sweden had long given her the control of the Balance of Power in the north. In every election for the Polish crown the King of Sweden had either sought ' the electoral honor for himself or had made his support essential in choosing the successful candidate.

Another reason urged Augustus of Saxony, the newly elected King of Poland, to curb the hated "imperialism" of Sweden. So unpopular was this German prince in his elective kingdom that he welcomed any opportunity for a foreign war which would turn the attention of his Slav subjects from internal affairs. Certain of victory in this enterprise he even took steps to reserve the honors of the promised campaign for the detested bodyguard of German troops who had accompanied him from Saxony. But the King of Poland and the Tsar were to learn that Charles of Sweden, in spite of his youth, was the first military genius of his age and that he commanded the most perfectly drilled and disciplined army in the north.

In the course of a single brilliant campaign Charles drove the King of Poland from the province of Lithuania. The Russians who had meanwhile advanced towards the Baltic were thrown into consternation by these events. At his leisure Charles now inflicted upon the Tsar's troops a great defeat at Narva. This victory, the more humiliating because even Peter's personal bravery was involved through stories of his cowardly conduct during the battle, also threatened the Russians' confidence in the value of the military reforms he had been at so much pains to introduce in place of their old drill and tactics. Meanwhile, isolated from his subjects by the intrigues of Piper (Charles' great foreign minister, whose diplomacy was almost as redoubtable as his master's sword) the King of Poland had become a dishonoured fugitive in his own dominions. The new candidate imposed upon the Poles in the person of Stanislaus Lesezynski was but a docile representative of the real King – Charles of Sweden.

But the genius of Peter the Great never displayed itself so brilliantly as after these disasters. "The Swedes," he repeated again and again, "will soon teach us how to fight." Gathering a new army he attempted to intervene on behalf of the deposed Saxon elector Charles easily crushed their united efforts at Altranstadt (1706). Even the electoral dominions of Saxony were now threatened and Augustus, in order to save his German possessions, was obliged formally to renounce all pretensions to the throne of Poland.

So threatening was the danger that he consented at the bidding of Charles to write a letter of congratulation to his successor, Lesezynski. Peter nevertheless resolved to continue the contest.

In the long struggle between Russia, Poland and Sweden that ensued, success almost invariably attended the armies of Charles XII. During this period the fortunes of Sweden were carried to their highest pinnacle. Historians now see that the "Mad King's" resolve to shatter the yoke of Moscovite influence in Poland by striking at the heart of Peter's vast empire, was more than a military adventure. The success of such a plan would have safeguarded the new Swedish possessions along the Baltic and established upon a lasting foundation his scheme, now all but realized, of making Sweden the supreme arbiter of the north.

But in the nine years which had elapsed since the battle of Narva, Charles had expended Sweden's hoarded treasure of men and money. Raw recruits now weakened the ranks of the veteran regiments he had inherited from his father. Youthful pride and obstinacy had induced him to discard the prudent ministers whose advice had been of such advantage in the earlier years of his reign. Charles might, with every advantage, have accorded the peace which the Tsar so earnestly desired in order to carry out his great plan of internal reform. He, nevertheless, continued active preparations for a new campaign. With the approach of the invading Swedish armies twenty thousand Cossacks were summoned by Peter to join in the defense of the Ukraine. His emissaries found the Cossack settlements in a state of almost open rebellion. A tax of seventy kopecks (no small sum of money in that day) had recently been placed upon every Cossack, not excepting those who were performing military service – an act bitterly resented as an infringement of the rights they had been assured at the time of their voluntary subjection to Russia. In Peter's plans for an accurate census of the Ukraine the Cossacks saw only a plan for fresh taxations and even more onerous terms of military service.

By thus overriding privileges of the Ukraine, Peter had aroused the resentment of both Cossack and non-Cossack inhabitants. Both classes felt themselves subjected for the first time to the same treatment as the despised *moujik* population of Great Russia – the serfs of the great administrative class favored by Peter's "reforms." Mazeppa as hetman of the Cossacks of the Ukraine had for many years been accorded nearly all the honours of an independent prince. Secure in Peter's favour, which he had enjoyed ever since the siege of Azov, he had looked forward in his old age to the easy enjoyment of this lucrative post. He now saw himself forced to take sides in a quarrel the probable outcome of which would only rivet more tightly the yoke of Russian imperialism on the inhabitants of the Cossack provinces. In the crisis now confronting him he took refuge in a time-honoured ruse. Although a half century of warlike service had till now seemed to weigh but lightly upon the veteran *hetman*, at Peter's summons he seemed suddenly overtaken by all the ills of deferred old age. For weeks at a time he remained in bed invisible to his followers, or else, propped in a great chair, supported by numerous cushions, he only received the Cossack officers to accept their condolences and to issue orders in the feeble voice of a valetudinarian. In expiation of past sins he commenced the construction of a great church, and to his former boon companions, expressed the edifying sentiment that "his thoughts were wholly withdrawn to the affairs of another life."

Nevertheless, in careful fulfillment of his duties as hetman he appeared to make every effort to furnish the Tsar with the levies of troops required. These were placed under the command of a Cossack colonel named Apostol. Although all these measures were taken in Mazeppa's name and he appeared zealously preparing to oppose the invasion of the Swedes, it seems equally certain, that at the same time constant negotiations were carried on with the emissaries of Charles. Offers of freedom and autonomy for the Ukraine were freely made by the Swedish monarch: Mazeppa's place was assured as the head of an independent state guaranteed by the armies of Charles. At last the *hetman* consented to enter into open revolt against the Tsar. In order to act with more certainty he suddenly quitted his rôle of an invalid and placed himself at the head of the Cossack armies. Appearing to yield to the urgent appeals of the Russian generals, he ordered all his *polki* to cross the Polish frontier.

Charles does not appear to have rated very high the military ability of the troops recruited among the Cossacks and peasant-proprietors of Little Russia. He was anxious, however, to secure a base for supplies for his own armies and guides for the vast unmapped country of the Ukraine, where he intended to develop his campaign. Perhaps the weakest feature of Charles' plans was his dangerous confidence in the ability of his veterans to overthrow almost any number of Russian troops which could be brought against him. But as the Cossack *polki* were only needed as auxiliaries, Mazeppa was instructed to maintain his fellow countrymen in a state of "discontent" – a none too difficult task!! – without definitely engaging himself until the last moment.

The hetman's position was, however, soon complicated by the constant reports which his rivals forwarded to the capital in order to convince the Tsar of his disloyalty. At first Peter was deaf to all such rumours, believing that Mazeppa in his old age would never betray a confidence he had done so much to deserve. As a fresh proof of his belief in the hetman's loyalty the Tsar sent back to the Ukraine bound in heavy chains, the principal agents of the malcontents who had undertaken the long journey to Moscow in order to denounce their chief. Thus perished two of the *hetman*'s oldest comrades in arms, Iska, a colonel of the Cossacks of Poltava, devoted to the cause of Russia, and Koutchebey, chief of one of the most important families of the Ukraine. These chieftains who had been the first to discern Mazeppa's intended treachery, would have been spared by the hetman if they would join his side, but scorning to save their lives at such a cost, both were now put to a shameful death with heavy blows from a poleaxe before the assembled *polk* and their own fellow townsmen.

For a brief time Mazeppa appears again to have wavered, perhaps touched by this display of loyal confidence on the part of a master he was about to betray. In his indecision he decided to summon a council of the Cossack notables, and himself proposed that a deputation be sent to Moscow to lay before the Tsar the grievances of the Ukraine. But Peter, growing suddenly suspicious, appears to have acted at this critical moment with the hasty violence which so often marred his statesmanship. His reply to the Cossack representatives was to throw into prison the entire deputation, at whose head the hetman had placed his favourite nephew. At the same time one of the Tsar's ablest generals, Mentchikov, commanding the Russian troops stationed in Cossack territory, received strict orders to spare no effort to prevent any communication between the Swedes and Poles.

The tenor of these orders persuaded Mazeppa that his treacherous negotiations were known and he could hesitate no longer without endangering his own safety. Placing garrisons chosen from the Cossacks of his faction in Romni, Tchernigov and Baturnin – thus securing important strategic points protecting his rear – he now advanced into Poland to join the Swedish armies, although keeping his intentions secret from those of his followers of whose loyalty he had reason to be doubtful. On the shores of the Desna, he drew up his entire army in a hollow square and in an impassioned harangue set forth their common wrongs. Appealing to the loyalty of the Cossack nation, he made the most of Peter's conduct respecting the ominous military reforms, recalling the Tsar's contempt for the agreements which, since the days of the Hetman Bogdan, had united Moscow and the Ukraine. But Mazeppa had either miscalculated the resentment which had been aroused by these measures, or, as appears more likely, the Cossacks hesitated to ally themselves with their ancient enemy, Poland. When thus called upon to forego at a few moments' notice the traditions and resentments of a life-time, they may have remembered that Mazeppa himself was of Polish origin. Their turbulent Orthodoxy caused them to recall all that their ancestors had suffered at the hands of the Catholic gentry and Jesuit leaders of the Polish court. The result of Mazeppa's ill-timed frankness was far different from his expectations. At first a grim silence greeted his eloquence, while murmurs of disapproval followed each new proposal. As he ended his appeal to Cossack prejudice, cries of "Treason" were heard on all sides. In the uproar that followed Mazeppa even appears to have had some difficulty in escaping from the violence of the Russian partisans among his excited followers.

With but two regiments remaining loyal, both belonging to his personal guard, his "invasion" of Poland became little better than a flight from the Ukraine. Of all the "host" of Cossack cavalry with whom he had promised to await his allies upon the shores of the Desna there remained but a handful of horsemen, while the main body of the Ukrainians and Cossacks returned homewards to make their submission to the Tsar's generals. One consolation remained, however, to Mazeppa in his extremity. The famous Zaporogian Cossacks were by this time too deeply compromised by the wily hetman's intrigues to desert his cause and they now set forth in their usual tumultuous array to join Mazeppa's little army.

Realizing the importance of ensuring the loyalty of this important part of the Cossack community, the Tsar had in the early stages of the events just narrated forwarded a present of sixty thousand florins to the *sitch*. It had, however, pleased the independent humour of these warriors to keep the money sent by the Russians and at the same time to declare for Charles and his Polish allies. In the pages of Norberg's History a full account is given of these negotiations, wherein the customs of the once famous Zaporogian brotherhood appear in no very creditable light. Their "war" leader, or *koshevoy ataman*, was, at this time, a Cossack named Gordianko. This worthy had but a short time before narrowly escaped massacre in the course of the tumultuous public assembly which had elected him to his office – a fact for which he held the envoys of the Tsar responsible. It was the recollection of this incident which may have disposed him so warmly to adopt the cause of the Hetman Mazeppa. At a meeting held in a secret spot on the shore of the Dikanka the temporary submission of the Zaporogians to the Hetman of the Ukraine had been agreed upon. The horse-tail standards of the Zaporogians had been dipped before the national flag of the Ukraine, and Mazeppa in an eloquent speech pointed out the necessity of an alliance against the Tsar. In order formally to celebrate the accession of the Zaporogians to the "Cossack cause" a banquet was now served to the delegates from the *sitch*. Around a board furnished with a magnificent service of silver plate (borrowed for the occasion from a Polish gentleman among Mazeppa's retinue) the Zaporogians renewed their solemn oath of allegiance to the cause of Charles XII and the Polish party with whom he was in alliance. On leaving the tent where these ceremonies had taken place the Zaporogian delegates were found to be in a state of complete drunkenness. Some of the more intoxicated even insisted on taking away the silver plates and goblets as a souvenir of the occasion saying that this was a Zaporogian's privilege. An unfortunate butler in an ill-advised attempt to save his master's property aroused the anger of these turbulent guests and was seized and stabbed to death. Not content with thus vindicating their injured dignity, the noble Zaporogians now declared through their *Koshevoy* that if they were not allowed to keep this spoil, according to ancient custom, they would immediately break off the newly-formed union to which they had engaged their followers. The matter was satisfactorily arranged, but during a subsequent interview with the King of Sweden it was considered wise to exact a promise from the Zaporogian envoys to "refrain from getting drunk before the banquet." It was upon the caprice of such allies that Charles depended to overthrow the power of Peter the Great! In the meantime, Mentchikov, the Tsar's favourite, had not been idle. As we have already observed the Russian troops had for some time been preparing for the not unexpected defection of Mazeppa and the Zaporogians. Shortly after the *hetman's* departure, Mazeppa learned that his own household, together with all the provisions he had amassed there for the winter campaign of the Swedish army, had been captured by a brilliant Russian attack. To serve as an example the Cossack notables of the town were put to death by Mentchikov with every refinement of cruelty. On the same scaffold perished a famous Cossack colonel named Glutchov and a Prussian officer named Koenigseck who had acted as the Cossack Chief of Artillery. At the same time an effigy of Mazeppa was vicariously "tortured" and solemnly degraded from the rank of hetman while a cross of St. Andrew was torn from the mannikin's breast. A more effectual punishment than this childish mummery was the solemn anathema launched against the hetman by the metropolitan of Kiev, a terrible indictment which included all the Orthodox Cossacks who were fighting with the heretics against the head of the Russian church.

As in the case of the rebellious Donskoi, the lacerated bodies of the most important of Mazeppa's adherents were placed on rafts and sent adrift on the Dnieper, so that the news of the Tsar's vengeance might be spread along the whole course of that stream.

At the famous battle of Poltava, whose course and the momentous results it entailed have so often been described, the Cossack nation again found itself hopelessly divided. The majority of the Cossacks and "free citizens" of the Ukraine fought under the banners of the Tsar, their oppressor. On the side of Charles XII the Zaporogians and the hetman's faithful regiments distinguished themselves in a last vain blow for the liberties of the Ukraine. But the armies of Sweden, until now victorious against Russian troops, were for the first time definitely defeated. The Tsar's troops, thoroughly drilled after the European model and his generals schooled in adversity, were at last able to prove their worth and the value of Peter's patient training. Russia's natural allies, cold and distance, added completeness to a defeat which anticipated the appalling disaster which overtook Napoleon a century later. Russia, not Sweden, became the preponderant power in the north of Europe, while, except for sporadic mutinies, little more was heard of the "liberties of the Ukraine" until the present day. The conduct of Mazeppa, whose miscalculations had destroyed one of the chief factors upon which Charles' strategy had been based, now gives the lie to those who see in his character only the acts of a finished opportunist. Accompanied by some three thousand Cossacks, Mazeppa and Charles (who, in spite of an agonizing wound had directed the battle from a bed borne on a litter of pikes) fled towards Turkey. The indomitable spirit of the "Lion of the North" still dreamed of rallying Sweden's broken armies. His plan was now to join the troops of General Loewenhaupt, who were waiting the king's arrival somewhere on the

Bessarabian border. On the shores of the Dnieper, the fugitives were thrust by their followers into a leaky boat and with an escort of about a dozen men abandoned to the swollen stream. Such was their peril that, in order to save themselves from sinking, the greater part of the hetman's treasure was thrown into the river.

At the same time a terrible fate overtook a large body of Swedish and Cossack cavalry who sought to cross the flooded Dnieper by swimming their horses in a compact mass, following the methods of the ancient Tartar invaders. Near the middle of the river this living raft became broken apart and the struggling horsemen met a terrible death among the rocks and rapids. Swept along by the ice floes of the treacherous stream their bodies accompanied the flight of their chief and the Hetman Mazeppa towards their exile in Turkish territory.

A few days later the fugitive learned of the defeat of the army commanded by Loewenhaupt. Continually pressed by Mentchikov's cavalry this general had finally been forced to surrender; fourteen thousand veteran Swedes laying down their arms to less than nine thousand Russians. The days when Charles' troops, as at Narva, had not hesitated to attack a force of Russians double or treble their own strength were ended. This victory was a final disaster to the Cossack faction devoted to Mazeppa. Mentchikov refused to include in the armistice and terms of surrender any amnesty for the Cossack partisans found among the Swedish armies. All who could not escape were massacred on the river bank "within sight of their fatherland," while the rest, according to the Tsar's orders, were relentlessly hunted down "in their lairs."

After this execution only three thousand Zaporogian warriors remained of all that famous brotherhood. On the approach of the Tsar's troops, these were forced to seek shelter among their ancient enemies the Turks. Realizing the value of such allies the Khan of the Crimean Tartars welcomed them in his camp, in spite of the wrong they had done his territory in the past. In order to show the Russians that they had definitely passed under Ottoman protection he conferred upon Mazeppa and the Zaporogian Hetman Gordianko the insignia of Turkish generals. lands were also set apart for the Zaporogians on the shores of the Koninke, where in ancient time the sitch or encampment of the free republic had been located.

The unfortunate hetman, Mazeppa, did not long survive his disgrace. With the feeble Cossack escort which had remained faithful to his cause he took refuge (still accompanied by the King of Sweden) at Bender under the protection of the Sultan of Turkey. Here his last days were constantly troubled by the fear that he might be delivered up to the agents of the Tsar. For losing sight of more immediate advantages, Peter now showed himself determined to secure the person of the old comrade in arms who had so traitorously deserted him. But the Ottoman Sultan, in spite of bribes of money and offers even more advantageous, remained loyal to the Cossack chieftain. In their misfortune, a warm friendship appears to have united Mazeppa and the fallen hero Charles.

All through the last illness of the former hetman, the young monarch continued to encourage the dying veteran with hopes of future success and revenge. Although Charles after a series of extraordinary adventures was at last restored to his native land, Mazeppa was unable to bear the double weight of years and misfortune. At the age of eighty he died in the Turkish camp without learning of the disaster which soon after overtook his great enemy the Tsar, in the full tide of his success at the battle of the Pruth.

THE END OF THE FREE UKRAINE: LITTLE RUSSIA

NOT the least important result of the battle of Poltava was the subjection of the greater part of the Free Ukraine to the will of the Russian crown. Although a majority of the Cossack inhabitants had refused to follow the lead of Mazeppa and might, therefore, have maintained in all fairness their rights to a continuation of the old privileges, the determination of Peter the Great to carry out his unifying reforms soon set definite bounds to the autonomy of the "settlements."

Even those most loyal to the Russian alliance could not see without sorrow the abrogation of privileges which dated from the days of Bogdan. Moreover, even in the most Russianized districts, the Tsar's suspicion of these turbulent, half-alien subjects soon led to further vexations and laws restricting their ancient Cossack liberties.

Peter's first act, after a strong military occupation had secured the imperial hold, was to require of the hetman and the principal Cossack dignitaries an oath of allegiance identical in form to that imposed upon the majority of his subjects. Henceforth the Tsar was legally "Autocrat" and the Ukraine became officially known by the hateful title as "the Province of

Little Russia."

At the same time a demand was made upon each of the Cossack polki or regiments for a contingent of men to be incorporated among the troops of the Russian army. By this means it was clearly indicated that the Cossacks of the Ukraine were now considered liable to regular military service like any other subjects of the empire. This policy also effectually weakened the power of resistance which the regiments furnished by the stanitzi might have opposed to Peter's "reforms" had they remained at their full strength.

In order to accentuate the changes which the old "Free Cossack" régime had suffered separate courts of justice were established at Joukhoff to administer the new Russian law instead of the old Cossack law based upon the "Institutes of Magdeburg." The only appeal from this tribunal lay in the courts of the empire and not, as heretofore, in the great Cossack reunions or the Council of Elders of each stanitza.

Meanwhile, in his camp at Bender, sometimes treated by the Turk as a distinguished prisoner, again consulted as an ally, Charles XII continued his intrigues against the Tsar and his vehement appeals to the powers of Europe to be allowed to return to his kingdom.

After the death of Mazeppa, Charles had continued on terms of friendly intimacy with Peter Orlick, who had been elected Hetman of the Zaporogians. The new chief of the former Free Republic was now wholly under the influence of his Turkish patrons. Although such base sycophancy offended the turbulent orthodoxy of his companions, Orlick affected even the dress of the Ottoman protectors. In order to make his position more secure, he also married a Tartar woman chosen in the seraglio of the Khan of the Crimea. His conduct could not fail to widen the breach which already existed between the Zaporogians and the Cossacks of the Ukraine.

But Peter still viewed with suspicion the border population of his new province. Any Cossack suspected of intercourse with the Zaporogians was cruelly put to death or transported to the pestilential marshes of Lake Ladoga, where tremendous drainage works were in progress in the neighbourhood of the new capital. This harsh treatment aroused widespread discontent throughout the Ukraine, and aware of this spirit of revolt, both the Turks and Zaporogians were encouraged to attempt once more an invasion of the Russian frontier.

In furtherance of this scheme, the diplomats of the Porte and the Grand Vizir of the Khan of Tartary pretended to treat the Zaporogians as an independent power. In a manifesto widely distributed among the villages of the old Ukraine the Cossacks were called upon to return to their Polish allegiance. The Turks not only promised to reestablish the rights of the Zaporogians, but also offered to assist the Cossack settlements along the upper Dnieper to regain their former freedom, if they would openly resist the oppressions and exactions of the Russians.

An expedition was next set on foot by the Porte wherein thirty thousand picked Tartar and Turkish troops were to join with Orlick and his Zaporogians in an invasion of the Russian and Polish Ukraine. In the same army was included a contingent of Poles disaffected by the Tsar's treatment of their country, under the leadership of a powerful noble of the ancient house of Pototski.

During this skilfully planned political-military campaign – wherein the diplomacy of Charles is plainly visible – orders were given to spare the Poles and Cossacks of the invaded districts while punishing without mercy the Russian troops and their adherents. This scheme, however, did not coincide with the time-honoured methods employed by the Tartars in their warfare. The subjects of the Khan and the even less disciplined Zaporogians soon began to indulge their talents for ruthless pillage, and following a few slight military successes in the beginning of the campaign, the allied armies dispersed in search of plunder. This enabled these scattered bands to be easily defeated by regular Russian troops under Prince Galitzine near Kiev. Their losses in battles and skirmishes are placed as high as five thousand.

While the Zaporogians and their Cossack allies were thus wasting a last opportunity to recover the freedom of the Ukraine, a body of picked Tartar troops, under the command of the Khan in person, succeeded in penetrating in a compact mass to the heart of Russian territory as far as Vorentz. The horrors of this invasion, recalling the excesses of the Tartar hordes under Batu Khan, rallied many districts wavering in their loyalty to Peter's standard. The principal military result of the expedition was obtained at Samara, where the Khan succeeded in destroying the Russian shipyards and a half-built flotilla, by means of which the Tsar had planned to descend the river Dnieper in an attempt to transfer the seat of war to the frontier of the Ottoman dominions. This feat of arms was probably responsible in part for the disastrous results of the famous Pruth campaign, upon which Peter now embarked at the instance of the Hospodars of the Christian provinces of Moldavia and Wallachia.

The events of this strange crusade, the most critical incident in Peter's career, do not belong to the subject in hand. It is sufficient to remark that his ill-prepared expedition cost Peter in the course of a few weeks, not only the prestige won through his defeat of the invincible armies of Charles of Sweden, but also placed him for a time at the entire mercy of his Turkish enemies. Had it not been for the fascinations and diplomacy of his new wife, the Empress Catherine, and the wholly unexpected clemency of the Turkish vizir, Tsar Peter – no longer "the Great" – would probably have ended his career a prisoner in Constantinople.

At the cost of nearly all the ready money in his treasury, a dearly won military reputation and a disastrous treaty, the emperor of all the Russias was at last enabled to return to his dominions – in spite of the frenzied protests of the Swedish king.

By the humiliating terms of the temporary peace of Falksen, which closed these "negotiations," the Russians returned the fortresses of Azov and Taganrog, commanding the littoral of the Black Sea, to the Turks. In the same document they promised not to infringe the "liberties" of the Cossacks of Poland nor those under the protection of the Khan of Crimea. But these advantages the Zaporogians enjoyed for only a brief period. By the terms of the Treaty of Pruth a more regular arrangement, far less favourable to the Free Cossacks, was concluded between the Tsar, the Khan of Crimea and the Porte. The Tsar was allowed to keep Kiev, together with the castles and fortified places defending the surrounding provinces as far south as Samara and Orel. To the "Free Cossacks" was assigned a territory with vaguely defined boundaries, forming a buffer state between the Southern province belonging to the Tsar and the Turkish provinces of the Black Sea and the Crimean littoral. A final clause, highly galling to the national susceptibilities of the brotherhood, engaged the Tsar on one hand and the Khan and Sultan on the other to repress and punish any invasion by the Zaporogians across the borders of the territory set aside for their use. These measures were fatal to Orlick's dream of an independent Cossack principality and put an end for the time being to further military activities on the part of his turbulent followers.

Although the Zaporogians had voluntarily sought the protection, rather than an alliance with, the Turks and Tartars, and could therefore hope for no special favours from these traditional enemies, – they appear nevertheless to have felt greatly aggrieved at their treatment. A special cause of complaint was the too ready acquiescence of their commander, Orlick, in every new requirement of the Turks. The Hetman, in order to remain in favour with the Porte, even consented to allow the Cossacks to be deprived of their artillery, while constant drill and reviews enforcing the irksome Turkish discipline in their ranks were looked upon as an infringement of their easy-going "military privileges." Although the Free Companions were soon weary of an alliance or tutelage which so estranged them from their fellow-Cossacks in Russia, during the lifetime of Peter the Great their overtures of peace were treated with contempt. It was not until the year 1732 that events occurred which caused a modification in Russia's policy towards them. On the death of Augustus II (to whom the Tsar had given the crown of Poland after Poltava), the Polish republic had relapsed into the customary state of anarchy which preceded the election of every new candidate to the vacant throne. Another king, Augustus III, was soon imposed upon the Poles by the Russian armies. Resenting this act of arbitrary power, a party among the Polish nobility and peasants now resolved once more to ask for the help and intervention of the Tartars and Cossacks.

In view of the possibility of such an invasion, the ministers of the Empress Ann were more ready than their predecessors to negotiate with the Zaporogians. A Russian officer visited the Zaporogian camp with regalia and presents for the *ataman* and the chiefs of the *Kourens*. . Not only was an invitation extended to the "Free Companions" to return to their old allegiance, and to re-establish the sitch on Russian territory, but a present of several million roubles was also offered towards the rebuilding and equipment of their camp below the cataracts of the Dnieper.

In order to counteract the success of these negotiations, the Sultan sent messengers from Constantinople charged with even richer presents than those offered by the diplomats of the Russian mission. But the Cossack leaders repulsed the Turkish overtures with scorn, and, loud in their expressions of attachment to the Orthdox Church and the Russian cause, sent the Pasha back to Constantinople with a negative reply. An untoward incident, however, marred the dignity of this noble action and the patriotic alliance which it sealed. No sooner had the Turkish envoy reached the limits of the Ottoman dominions, than he was set upon by a company of Zaporogians, who had secretly followed his march till he had crossed the borders where the laws of hospitality protected him. The returned presents were then carried back as booty to the *sitch*. While disavowing this action, by a characteristic process of reasoning the Zaporogians nevertheless decided that the goods involved must now be considered "fair-prize," and as such they were duly divided among the entire company!

In order to give immediate proof of their zeal for the Russian alliance, thus irretrievably renewed, a raid was forthwith undertaken upon the ill-starred provinces of the Polish frontier. The indiscriminate massacre which ensued warned the Russians of the dangers of allowing too much liberty to the Zaporogians. The government took measures to restrict in many ways the famous "liberties" of the sitch. Thus the "Free Companions" were forced for the first time to accept the control of a Russian officer stationed in their midst, while a council made up of three Russians and three Cossacks was placed in command of the territories assigned to them in the Ukraine. It will readily appear from the preceding paragraphs that the old characteristics of the sitch — a border garrison drawn from the Cossack frontier settlements of the Ukraine as a protection against the raids of Tartars – had by this time wholly disappeared. The Zaporogians had become in the course of time little more than an organized band of border ruffians, anxious only to sell their services to the best advantage. Their conduct during the years of their association with the Porte had moreover estranged them from their old neighbours. It is even doubtful whether the true "Cossacks" in their ranks represented any element but the offscourings and incorrigibles of the Ukrainian Cossack villages and farmsteads.

The last occasion on which the Zaporogians were regularly employed as auxiliaries by the Russian government was in the war which broke out between Russia and the Porte. The open violation of the Treaty of Pruth by Peter's successors, the Empresses Elizabeth and Ann, left no other course open to the Sultan but war. In the famous campaigns which ensued, planned by General Münnich, the Turkish provinces of the Black Sea and the territories of the Khan of the Crimea were overrun and devastated. Nearly eight thousand Zaporogians shared the difficulties and the privations of the expedition, and their knowledge of the peculiar tactics of desert warfare made them of great service.

At the siege of Ochakov; an operation carried on by land and sea, the Zaporogians constructed a fleet of their famous long boats and in these fragile craft boldly attacked the Turkish fleet. As at the siege of Azov, the disconcerting movements of this light flotilla succeeded in inflicting heavy damage upon the galleons of the enemy. The characteristic reward received for these actions is set down by Lesur in the following terms:

"Letters patent of 'satisfaction'; a great standard embroidered with the arms of Russia; a horsetail Cossack standard enriched with gold; an enamelled bundchuk or a mace for the *koshevoy*, and several millions of roubles as a gratification for the 'Free Companions.' At the same time Ann is reported to have caused herself to be inscribed as a member of the sitch – a strange distinction, indeed, for this womanless community."

However, by thus aiding in the destruction of their traditional foes, the Tartars of the Crimea, the Zaporogians had at the same time removed the principal reason for which their unruly garrison had so long been tolerated. The passing of frontier conditions along the borders of the Ukraine inevitably led to the disappearance of the Zaporogian sitch, the classic stronghold of Cossack liberties and traditions.

In 1768, in a last burst of "Zaporogian fury," the garrison of the *sitch* had fallen upon the hapless frontiers of the Polish Ukraine. "All who were not of the Greek religion, including old men, women, children, nobles, servants, monks, labourers, artisans, Jews, Catholics, Lutherans, were massacred without distinction. The entire province presented the appearance of a city taken by assault." (Lesur.)

The lust for plunder, masquerading under the excuse that their co-religionists were persecuted by the Poles, was the cause of this outrage. Such barbarity sent a thrill of horror through all the civilized courts of Europe. So great was the indignation that the Empress Catherine hastened formally to disclaim all responsibility for the behaviour of her Zaporogian subjects. Russian regular troops were sent to surround the isolated bands returning to the *sitch*, and besides depriving them of their loot, forced the majority of the best troops to enroll in the sternly disciplined Cossack *slovodni* regiments of the Ukraine. Only the outbreak of another Turkish war saved the *sitch* from further reprisals. A sudden attack by Turks and Tartars on the new frontier provinces, coinciding with the strange revolt of the wild Cossacks of the Asiatic frontier under Pougatchev – "the false Peter the

Third" – deferred this righteous execution.

Representations were, however, made to induce the Zaporogians "to conform to the laws of civilization." In vain they objected that their organization had always existed as it stood. Their peculiar discipline (or rather the lack of military rules) they justified by the successes of their tactics against the enemies of Russia. Forgetting their frequent disloyalties they invoked the ukases of former Tsars confirming them *perpetually* in their privileges. Their favourite threat when pressed by Catherine's officers was to pretend that they were about to return to their Turkish allegiance. Thus, while the war with the Sultan lasted, Catherine feared to punish their insolence.

But with the signing of the treaty of Kainardji the Empress turned her attention to reorganizing the Russian border provinces against a possible renewal of Turkish aggression. It was now decreed that the Zaporogian *sitch*, the focus of all disorders in the Ukraine, should disappear. Even the privilege of a spirited or heroic climax to their long career of disorder was to be denied them! A force of troops so overwhelming that to resist would have appeared madness, surrounded the stronghold on every side. Completely surprised and cowed by such a determined campaign the Zaporogians "without even bloodshed" surrendered their arms to the representatives of Catherine's authority. The *sitch* was declared "forever destroyed and the name of Zaporogian wiped out." In order the more effectually to ensure that no reorganization of their band might take place, the territory of the Zaporogians was divided among the neighbouring provinces of Little Russia and colonized with "foreigners." The lands once under the immediate control of the *sitch* now form part of the Russian "government," of Ekaterinaslav, Kherson and Tauride.

HISTORY OF THE COSSACKS

The conditions of the Cossacks living in the settlements or *stanitzi* of Little Russia differed but little at the end of the eighteenth century from that of the *Onodvortzi*, or peasant-proprietors of Greater Russia. From the account of contemporary writers, it would appear that the warlike qualities which formerly distinguished the Ukraine – fostered by a life of continual campaigning against their numerous enemies – had largely disappeared under the conditions brought about by the long- enforced peace following the firm establishment of Russian rule.

The old system of land tenure was fast disappearing and great estates had already been formed from Cossack land and granted to Russian and Polish nobles. Moreover at this time the ancient territory of the Free Ukraine was invaded on all sides by the advance of Russian colonists. An entire new province, known as New Servia, was thus settled on the Turkish frontiers with a population drawn from the Christian provinces of Turkey and peasants of Northern Russia. In order to establish these newcomers as quickly as possible, Catherine sent regiments of dragoons to plough and sow these fertile territories long uncultivated owing to fear of the Mussulman.

Internal change also threatened the characteristic civilization of the Cossacks of Little Russia. During the short-lived rule of Peter III an attempt was made to introduce a system of nobility among the officers of the Cossack regiments, undermining the democratic principle of equality which had formed one of the strongest traditions of Cossack life. Under Catherine the Great, even more strenuous measures were taken to wipe out all differences between the Ukraine and the neighbouring Russian provinces.

During the strange parliament summoned at Petrograd by the

Empress (in an access of what she flattered herself was "liberalism") we find "representatives" from the Ukraine Cossacks among the delegates forcibly gathered to deliberate upon a general system of laws for the "people" of Russia. Proud of their national customs and regulations, the Cossacks of the Ukraine appear to have strenuously resisted all these innovations. But the terrible Roumianzov, now Catherine's favourite minister, would not allow this imperial passion for reform to be denied. The delegates from the Cossack provinces were dragged to the capital in chains and forced to take part in the debates under the guard of Russian troops. As a result of their strange deliberations a new code of laws was adopted for the Ukraine, in Which the ancient customs of the Cossacks were given little consideration. Thus a new impetus was given the great migration of Cossacks towards the Caucasus and the Kouban – beyond the settlements of the Don – where their descendants have preserved their customs to the present day.

POUGATCHEV

AT no time since the *"Troublous Days"* which followed the death of Boris Godounov has the *padarok* or public order of the Russian people seemed so irretrievably disturbed as at the present time. The period of anarchy to which the above name was given has always been looked upon with pious horror by the *moujik*, at heart a none too heroic lover of peace and quiet above all other considerations. Yet the *"Red Terror"* of the present day is not the only grave upheaval which, since the days of the *"False Dmitri,"* has disturbed the slow evolution of Russia toward light and civilization. The strange "seeking" un-European idealism of the peasantry makes them liable – in spite of their instinctive docility – to almost savage outbreaks of impatience. Again and again false prophets have arisen to deceive the people. If true Russians, these have often deceived themselves.

Pougatchev, the leader of the great Cossack revolt during the latter half of the eighteenth century, was a typical specimen of the Russian mob-leader. In addition to ruthlessness and the gift of command he possessed talents of organization and military leadership which the Bolshevik chieftains of the present day might well envy. Above all he appears as a master of the note of religious appeal which in Russia must always accompany "popular" success – an appeal recalling the dominant note of Russian life, whether made in the name of a schism in the Orthodox Church, on behalf of some socialist doctrine like that preached to-day in the form of a gospel "according to Marx."

After the partition of Poland and the success of Catherine's armies during their Polish campaigns, every curious detail with respect to the vast empire governed by *"The Semiramis of the North"* was eagerly sought after and commented upon in the distant capitals of Europe. The correspondence which the Empress Catherine conscientiously maintained with Voltaire and Diderot, besides her letters to Grimm, her unofficial representative and accredited gossip in Paris – kept this extraordinary woman constantly before the eyes of her contemporaries. For in spite of their fine contempt for kings and kingship, the philosophers thus honoured were in no way averse to publishing the details of their literary intimacy with a powerful sovereign. Catherine, on the other hand, forever cut off by the circumstances of her position from the brilliant society she felt so well qualified to grace, seems to have been consoled by the thought that vicariously at least she had become known to the *salons* of Paris and London.

Social philosophy was the fashionable distraction of the hour. Like the *"Parlor-Bolsheviki"* of our own day, Catherine delighted in the parading before her literary friends principles of the most advanced and enlightened liberalism. Taking its tone from the *dilettante*'f reformers of the gardens of Versailles, the correspondence of the Empress-Autocrat is constantly concerned with the solution of problems concerning the welfare of her fellow-beings and the *"Rights of Man."* The news which she herself announced of the revolt of Pougatchev, bringing to the attention of these courtly republicans the stirring of mighty primitive forces in the depths of a wholly unknown Russia, came as a sensational bit of news to Catherine's correspondents. In the doings of the mysterious beings known as *"Cossacks"* they may perhaps have recognized the embodiment of that strange philosophical conception, *"Primitive Man,"* whose virtues were so lauded by their oracle, M. Rousseau. And the fact that the hardy rebel chieftain (the Cossack leader to whom Catherine refers as *"M. Pougatchev"*) actually claimed to be the husband of the Tsarina added an almost scandalous touch to a situation filled with every possibility of interest.

From the mass of exaggerations and fiction which have grown up about the great Cossack revolt and the person of Pougatchev we may now try to clear away some of the inaccuracies with which the legends of the Chap-Books have overlaid established facts. Yet even as set forth in the pages of the judicious historian of the Cossacks, Lesur, the barest report of these doings would seem hardly to require literary embellishment. "If audacity of character and conception – and excesses dictated by brutality and ferocity – can make a brigand worthy to figure in history, no one has more merited this deplorable honour than the subject of the present account." *("Histoire des Kosaques,"* Lesur.)

Yemelyan Pougatchev, generally known by the Russian diminutive of his name, *"Yemelka,"* was born about 1723 in the Cossack *stanitza*] of Zimovnikaja on the Don. Enrolled at an early age in the Cossack regiment to which this district was obliged to furnish its quota, he followed the campaigns and shared in the honors gained by Catherine's armies during the Seven Years' War and in the subsequent War of 1769 against the Turks. After the siege of Bender some difference with his military chiefs caused him to desert from the army. Taking refuge in Poland he was next heard from in a convent of the Greek Orthodox Church near the Russian border.

In the villages nearby the religious sectarians known as Baskolniki or *"Old Believers"* had established numerous "congregations." These fanatics represented the reactionaries or *"Puritans"* of the Russian Church. The principal tenet of their belief was an uncompromising resistance to the reforms which Peter the Great had introduced in the ritual of the Greek Orthodox Church. It is difficult to believe that the Cossack trooper Pougatchev had any deep knowledge of the finer points of this ecclesiastical controversy. His rebellious nature, however, found sympathetic fellowship with the *Raskolniki*, who, on account of continued refusal to conform to the government's decrees, either in political or religious matters, were subject to persistent persecution.

Above all else *"The Old Believers"* prided themselves in following with literal exactitude the teachings of the *Old Testament*. A favourite text among them was the verse setting forth that "among the followers of Christ there shall be neither first nor last." To this doctrine of absolute equality – travestied by the Bolshevik philosophy of our own day – they joined an almost Mohammedan conviction that to die for the faith was the highest form of happiness.

To stop the spread of Raskolnik doctrine all kinds of limitations had been placed upon the activities of their missionaries. In many places they were forbidden to own property, or when permitted to do so were forced to pay double taxes. In some towns it was enacted that, like Jews, the Raskolniki must wear clothing of a distinguishing colour and fashion. These measures had the usual effect of religious persecution: increasing both their zeal and numbers.

In the older provinces of the Ukraine the strong arm of the Orthodox Church, strengthened by the determination of Peter the Great to rule over a uniform and religiously "united" empire, reduced even the most fanatical opponent of his policy to silence or obedience. To the Puritan-minded Raskolniki existence in *"Holy Russia"* became intolerable.

In the remote provinces of *"New Russia,"* along the Asiatic frontier, especially among the Cossacks of the Jaik whose free traditions were opposed to any infringement of personal liberty, many Raskolniki who had fled for refuge found that their teaching met with particular success. It was probably in the company of one of these bands that Pougatchev emigrated to this congenial frontier atmosphere. Here he was assured of a welcome both as a Raskolniki and as a Cossack who had already suffered in the cause of liberty by resisting the harsh discipline of the *slovodi* of the Don.

Even allowing for a certain degree of religious sincerity in Pougatchev's beliefs, the course of conduct he now adopted tends to show that considerations of morality entered very little into his plans. Soon after his arrival among the *Jaikskoi*, Pougatchev became the chief of a mixed band of Cossacks and frontiersmen who, on the pretence of levying toll or passage money from the merchants travelling in the no-man's land near the River Kontai, in reality carried on depredations worthy only of a crew of bandits. For some time these strange Puritans continued to "spoil the Egyptians" with considerable success. In the end it was as a common highwayman, rather than on account of any dangerous "revolutionary" activities, that he earned the distinction of being arrested by the authorities and taken to Kazan for judgment. Soon after, through the carelessness of the Russian officials in charge of his prison and the aid of fellow-Raskolniki, he managed to escape.

Now began the career which has given to Pougatchev such strange and terrible notoriety. His plan was to return, with as little delay as possible, to the distant Cossack bands of the Jaik, where, among the malcontents of the frontier, he could resume his interrupted leadership. Disguised as a boatman he followed the great highway of the Volga and its tributaries until these carried him to a point where the settlements near the town of *Jaikskoi* could be reached.

His return came at an opportune moment. The Russian government had again attempted to introduce among the unruly inhabitants of this thinly populated province the same military reforms that had been imposed on the Cossacks of the Dnieper and Don. Besides the settlements of the ancient *Jaikskoi*, whose origin is traced from the remnants of Scythian tribes, Cossacks of the lower Jaik included large numbers of runaway Russian serfs and religious refugees. Above all else they were a liberty-loving race. Like all true frontiersmen the Jaik Cossacks held agriculture in small esteem. Cattle-herding, hunting and the rich fisheries of the river Ural furnished the means of a far easier existence. To these pleasant pursuits they added a profitable exploitation of the great natural salt fields found in the marshes of the river.

The Empress Catherine's policy was to build up in all her frontier provinces an agricultural population of peasant farmers. Although none of these foreign colonists were transferred to the Jaik, whole villages were settled about Samara on the Volga. But by this means new animosities were aroused, for in the process many of the original settlers were despoiled in favour of the newcomers. Most of the latter were, moreover, Germans, whose descendants, aliens in language and belief, were to be found, until the outbreak of the present war, living side by side with the Russian population, still divided from their neighbours by ancient quarrels.

At the same time that the Cossacks found themselves ousted from great tracts of "range" necessary for their cattle, the government had sought to force them to more "civilized pursuits" by cutting off the subsidies which had been allowed to every head of a Cossack family in return for his military services against the neighbouring Turkoman tribesmen. The strong element of Raskolniki among the Cossacks held to their beliefs with fanatical determination. These observances were often the cause of serious trouble with the authorities. Like the *boyars* of Peter's time, the sectarians refused, on religious grounds, to shave or "trim the corners of the beard." When the military authorities were ordered to enroll these matchless horsemen into regiments of *"Hussars"* for service during the Turkish war, the first act of the general in command (a German, one of many serving in the Russian armies) was to order that his bearded recruits be publicly shorn in the principal square of the town of *Jaikskoi*. His fixed belief that no hussar could fight unless wearing moustaches prescribed by the German regulations ended in the massacre of all the foreign officers engaged in recruiting service. Only the arrival of regular troops put an end to this mutiny. The leaders, enjoying the approval and support of the Cossacks, easily escaped to the neighbouring desert.

In their secret headquarters on the Kirghiz steppes, Pougatchev joined the leaders of this revolt. Although in the eyes of the Tsarina's officials Pougatchev was only an escaped convict, his prestige was now established among the *"Old Believers"* by the imprisonment he had suffered for his religious belief. Successful defiance of the regulations protecting the merchants on the caravan road was but an added title to their respect. Before long he found himself elected the leader of a band of desert *"Free Companions,"* who, with some pretence of copying the organization and customs of the Zaporogian Cossacks, now declared themselves independent of all authority. Travelling merchants and caravans were attacked under the pretext of levying toll on all who ventured across their territory. Organized "lifting" of the cattle belonging to their more peaceful neigbbours also furnished the means of an easy, even joyous, existence.

In the spring of the year 1773 Pougatchev, perhaps in order more formally to establish his leadership among his wild companions, or dreaming of wider opportunities for his ambition, appears first to have conceived the plan of appealing to their allegiance by claiming to be the murdered Tsar Peter III. Wildly improbable as the scheme may appear, it had, nevertheless, many features which promised success. The circumstances surrounding the assassination of this unworthy monarch, whom Catherine had supplanted, had always remained a disquieting mystery to the peasants of Russia. According to popular belief (but for what historical reasons it is difficult to determine) he was generally supposed to have suffered martyrdom on account of his devotion to the cause of the peasant reforms. Among the *"Old Believers"* and the other strange sects which flourished on the Russian borders, he was, moreover, greatly revered because of the leniency he had shown to their brethren during his brief and disordered reign. The manner in which the Empress had succeeded her unworthy husband on the throne had always been left unexplained by Catherine in her proclamations announcing this event in distant parts of the empire. The belief appears to have existed that the rightful Emperor was only held in prison by the officials devoted to Catherine and her favourites. Thus the rumour that *"Father Peter"* was still alive had probably long been current among the Cossacks of the Asiatic frontier before Pougatchev sought to turn the legend to his own advantage.

Pougatchev, for this device or impersonation, could not even claim originality. Only a century before the boy Tsarevitch Dmitri – murdered by his ambitious guardian, Boris Goudonov – had been successfully impersonated by a mysterious personage known in history under the name of the *"False Dmitri."* This was probably one Gregory Ostrepiev, a young monk who, with the support of the Polish nobility (whose credulity, in view of the questions of policy it involved, it is unnecessary to fathom), actually succeeded in revenging upon the son of the Russian usurper the crime to which the father owed the throne. For a few months Gregory ruled the distracted *Russian Empire as Tsar* (1606).

That the "fraud" of Ostrepiev did not result in establishing a new dynasty permanently upon the Russian throne seems rather due to the character of the new Tsar than to any doubts with respect to his legitimate rights. His advent as a force capable of restoring order in the midst of the *"Troublous Times"* had been hailed with delight by the whole Russian people. Had not Dmitri shown himself too Polish in his habits and taste to suit his new subjects, he would probably have reigned to the end of his days. But "because he ridiculed the monks and went bear hunting like the Polish king, the populace of Moscow struck him down, burning his body as that of a 'sorcerer' who had deceived the people."

The reign of the succeeding Tsar Shouiski (little more legitimate than the pretender who opposed him) was troubled by a whole series of *"False Dmitris."* One of these, a Donskoi Cossack, succeeded in backing up his pretensions with a Falstafflan army in whose ranks marched four or five fellow-pretenders, each impersonating some member of the imperial family.

It would seem highly probable that the traditions of these more or less successful impostors would have been preserved in the folk-songs and legends of the Don *stanitza* where Pougatchev was born. In turning their example to account by attempting to exploit the belated popularity of the ignoble husband of Catherine the Great, the bandit leader only followed a generally successful precedent well known in Cossack history.

From the beginning Pougatchev seems to have found little difficulty in inducing the majority of his companions to accept his pretensions to be Peter III, the rightful Tsar of Russia. While the Russian authorities treated with ridicule the bombast of the false "monarch" who, from his capital or encampment in the salt desert of Jaik, addressed them in pompous manifestoes, new recruits flocked to his standard in alarming numbers. Soon the Raskolniki and the element of discontented peasants and landless Cossacks, to whom his eloquence was generally directed, began to believe in the infallibility of this fierce desert Messiah. A few easily won military successes also added stability to his throne. Skilfully choosing as the object of his attacks the almost defenceless German colonists, established by Catherine near the Free Cossack lands, and therefore objects of particular hatred to the entire Cossack population, – he directed a popular crusade to restore this territory to the previous owners. His speedy triumphs were even tempered with a certain "royal" clemency. Leaving to his alien victims the bare necessities of existence; in return for a promised tribute and the acknowledgment of his imperial claims their lives were spared. At the same time a rich booty provided his followers with much needed stores and equipment to continue their campaign.

Along the course of the lower Jaik only the principal town, *Jaikskoi*, was able to resist the fury of Pougatchev's attack. When summoned to surrender "in the name of the Tsar," the leaders of the garrison replied that they were too familiar with the name of Pougatchev and the reputation of the ruffians composing his band even to consider such an impudent demand. In the face of this challenge, whether because he felt himself unprepared for a siege, or on account of the possible effect of the derisive rebuke he had received upon the allegiance of his followers, Pougatchev now returned to his desert stronghold, where he began busily recruiting his forces for an attack upon Orenburg, the principal town of the Russian frontier provinces.

The Governor of Orenburg was at this time an officer in the regular Russian army, newly arrived and without experience in desert warfare. Underestimating the force of a movement led by so ridiculous an individual as a "false Peter III" he angrily ordered the small garrison of the two nearest frontier outposts to proceed, without delay, against the rebels. By a series of lightning marches — such as only Cossack troops are capable of performing — Pougatchev succeeded in defeating first one and then the other of these detachments. The soldiers who volunteered to join his ranks were welcomed among the armies of the pretender. The remainder, including nearly all the officers, were pitilessly massacred. (When one recalls the composition of Catherine's frontier armies, the lifelong exile of the serf-soldiers and criminals who served out their penal sentences in its ranks, it is in no way surprising to learn that many disciplined recruits were gained by the rebels from prisoners and deserters from the imperial forces.)

Orenburg, the rich centre of an important group of caravan trails crossing the Turcoman deserts, although defended by a fortress and heavy earthen walls, was next attacked. Only the courageous conduct of the garrison of a neighbouring post whose defense delayed the advance of the Cossacks long enough to enable the governor to obtain reinforcements, saved the capital of Russia's Asiatic provinces from the fierce attack of Pougatchev's army.

Following the continued success of their leader, these had now become a force by no means to be readily dispersed. Besides a majority of the Jaikskoi Cossacks, Pougatchev had under his command a great body of

Bashkir tribesmen and several bands of unruly Budjiak Tartars who had but recently been exiled to these deserts from the Crimea by Catherine's orders. Eleven thousand Kalmoucks, after massacring the Russian officials set over them, joined his standard in a body. Even a detachment of Polish gentlemen and their retainers, exiles on their way to Siberia, lent him the aid of their military knowledge, burning to avenge on Catherine, by any means at hand, the wrongs she had inflicted upon their country.

Pougatchev now found his word the undisputed law over an empire geographically as vast as the Central Europe of to-day. In all this wide but sparsely settled territory only the garrisons of a few strongly fortified towns were able to hold out against his assaults. Had the Cossacks waited until hunger and despair brought about the surrender of these isolated garrisons, the results might have been different. But in order to maintain the military ardour of his followers, anxious for plunder, an active siege of Orenburg was undertaken. In full sight of the garrison of Orenburg, the Cossack leader carried out the reviews and ceremonies of his grotesque court, seeking by every means in his power to impress both upon his fickle subjects and the beleaguered enemy a sense of his new importance. The personality of Pougatchev had by this time become entirely merged in that of Peter III. Perhaps deluded by some strange doctrine of transsubstantiation, he appeared to have persuaded himself of the actual truth of his claims. His supporters among the Raskolniki enabled him to adopt the rôle of prophet as well as Tsar. Dressed in gorgeous pontifical robes he distributed absolution and blessings on his wild followers reduced to a state of reverential awe by these mummeries. (Pushkin's *"The Captain's Story,"* a piece of brilliant fiction founded on profound historical research, deals with these events.)

On his banners was inscribed in letters of gold the legend ""*Redivivus et ultor"* (Resurrected and avenging). About his person high-titled officers and attendants exercised their offices real and imaginary. At meals Polish noblemen, of authentic lineage, served him as lackeys. To the sound of trumpets and the beating of drums royal toasts were drunk – to the future of the "popular cause." In the government of his strange dominions a council of ministers, with the title of *boyars*, carried out his orders and issued *ukases* in due form. An order of chivalry was established which conferred grandiloquent titles upon Cossack peasants and Kalmouck braves. Pougatchev even succeeded in issuing a rough coinage bearing his effigy with the title *"Peter III Emperor of all the Russias."*

Had Pougatchev possessed the strength of character necessary to maintain the rôle he had first affected – that of a religious and social reformer – the forces of discontent might have gathered from all over Russia to his banners. The long-promised reforms, demanded by the peasants, had been but the amusement of Catherine's leisure. The endless formal enquiries and reports which she had caused to be drawn up with reference to taxation and peasant emancipation, and the "Congress" to which delegates were dragged, sometimes in chains, to listen to adulation of their mistress, were only intended by her courtiers to flatter the Tsarina's "liberalism." The signs of a deep-rooted discontent with the established order was everywhere apparent.

In spite of the grotesque pretensions which attended his career, Pougatchev's crusade against the nobles and landlords might have gathered a formidable following. Like the "False Dmitri," he now dreamed of Moscow and a throne in the Kremlin. The gravity of the situation which confronted Catherine was, to a certain degree, admitted. Proclamations in which she at last condescended to notice, and even argue, with respect to Pougatchev's claims to be Peter III now appeared. Although she wrote to

Voltaire of the doings of "Monsieur de Pougatchev," she was, nevertheless, careful at the same time to warn her subjects "to obey only the laws signed by my own hand." An appeal was also made to the Cossacks of the Jaik to return to their true allegiance.

A measure far more dangerous to the cause of the pretender was an offer of a tremendous reward (100,000 roubles) to be paid for his person or proof of his death. Pougatchev, who could neither read nor write, caused a series of manifestos to be issued in answer to these *ukases* promising among other reforms freedom of the serfs and restoration of all Cossack privileges. This was a political move of no little sagacity. Even in the distant parts of European Russia Pougatchev's "program" was everywhere greeted with enthusiasm.

The chief danger to Pougatchev's cause was now to arise from his own natural ferocity of character and the unbreakable chains of brutal passions. Imagining that his kingly state was now assured, he allowed himself to indulge with impunity in the most outrageous debauchery. His conduct soon became a cause for scandal among the Raskolnik elders who had formed his first disciples. The "unco guid" of the Cossack community – rigid followers of the text of the ancient Scriptures – might condone acts of freebooting and piracy which could be considered in accordance with the divine ordinance to "spoil the Egyptians," but the spectacle which their leader soon afforded them, and especially his amorous subjection to a notorious harlot of Jaikskoi, lost him the support of these rigid sectarians. When he insisted on the presence of the elders at a wedding feast with "Jezebel" (for in spite of the fact that he had a legally wedded Cossack wife, he was bent upon celebrating a fresh alliance by an orgy worthy in every respect of his bride), a mutiny occurred among his followers. In order to distract the attention of his army from these troublesome domestic matters he now threatened to lay siege in regular form to the great city of Kazan, and a strong Russian force under General Bibikov was sent to the relief of that place.

By a quick march towards the frontier, Samara, an important city on the Volga, was recovered from the rebels, and the lower course of this stream once more opened to navigation. But the wild character of the country, among whose deserts and salt marshes his followers found themselves at home, enabled "Peter III" not only to keep his armies intact, but also to obtain a sudden advantage. Returning after a long détour, he surprised an isolated force forming the personal guard of General Bibikov. Amazed by this unexpected attack the Russians were almost annihilated and their leader escaped, only to die later of a slight wound, which his rage and mortification alone rendered serious.

Galitzine and his regulars now once more appeared upon the scene, attacking the Cossack bands with such vigour that in the course of a six hours' struggle the rebels were in their turn completely defeated. This time, Pougatchev with a few followers barely succeeded in escaping to the unknown country among the foothills of the Urals. Through the success of these military operations the great Cossack rebellion was generally supposed in Europe to be at an end. But the cause of Pougatchev had become identified with the wrongs of the peasants, the sufferings of the enforced colonists of the Siberian frontier and the "privileges" of which the Cossacks felt themselves unjustly deprived. Even the wild tribes of Bashkirs and Kalmoucks inhabiting the deserts and steppes about Orenburg looked to Pougatchev to relieve them of the taxes and tasks imposed upon them by Catherine's officers. His misfortunes, moreover, had done much to wipe out the unfavourable impression made by his excesses in the minds of the Puritan Raskolniki. In ever-increasing numbers recruits once more travelled by desert ways, unknown to the Russians, to join the new "Army of Revenge." Fanaticized by his indomitable eloquence and energy, his wild horsemen made a sudden descent upon the frontier blockhouses undeceiving the officials who had thought Pougatchev's powers for mischief-making at an end.

This time the help of one of Russia's ablest generals, Michelson (a soldier of Scottish descent, the favourite pupil of the great Romarzov), was invoked to meet the situation. Wholly new tactics were adopted. Quantities of mounted troops were improvised from the foot regiments, and during a running battle of three days Michelson finally succeeded in cornering his enemy. A'crushing defeat put an end to the strange career of the Cossack "Peter III" – *"redivivus"* no more. Pougatchev escaped, but veteran troops, including several regiments of Cossacks from the Don lately returned from the Turkish wars, were now used by the Russian authorities to hunt down the scattered bands of the malcontents. A last tragic episode was, however, to be added to the ill-fame of the chieftain.

The wrongs of the dispossessed Cossacks and peasants who formed a large part of Pougatchev's armies, justified in a measure their actions and their revolt against tyranny. But no cause, however just, could long prosper under such a leader. To the last, the career of the "Cossack Tsar" remains unrelieved by a single ray of noble or generous intention. Seldom was a popular "hero" so unworthy of his opportunities. The news of the final defeat of Pougatchev's armies was coupled with that of a brutal murder which, even in his retreat, he paused to accomplish. The philosopher Lowitz, who, with a few learned companions, had been engaged in surveying a route for a canal to join the great highway of the Volga with the Black Sea, was surprised by the fleeing "Tsar Peter" during this work. The celebrated *savant* – to give point to a brutal jest – was impaled upon a long stick "in order to continue star gazing."

Pougatchev's intemperate and brutal nature was also the cause of his final capture. In spite of the reward set upon his head, three faithful companions had shared with him the dangers and privations of his flight. While lurking in hiding among the salt lakes not far from the Jaik, one of these three — overcome by fatigue and the hopelessness of their situation — dared to suggest to his chief the advisability of considering a surrender. Pougatchev, perhaps thinking to overawe his comrades, without hesitation drove his dagger into the speaker's throat.

The companions of the murdered man now threw themselves on their leader and binding him with his own horse's reins and bridle, carried him to the Russian troops under General Zaharov, commanding the town of Jaikskoi. From this place, which had been the scene of "Peter III's" wildest exploits and excess successes, he was carried to Moscow in an iron cage, a species of terrible show and example to all the villages along the way.

In captivity Pougatchev showed the psychological transformations so common to wild and brutal natures. His jailers and those who visited him in his prison were astonished to find, instead of the terrible monster created by popular belief, a mild and cringing convict continually hopeful of a reprieve.

Yet the extraordinary powers of persuasion or personal magnetism of which the Cossack leader was master were to be exercised even upon his executioner. The sentence passed upon the "False Peter the Third" — no more barbarous than his crimes demanded in the opinion of his time — required that "he should be quartered alive, his hands and feet cut off, and his ashes then to be thrown to the winds." As a last grace the public hangman consented on the scaffold to alter the course of this terrible punishment, moved by Pougatchev's tears and eloquent pleadings. First cutting off the bandit's head at a single blow, he thus mercifully ended his sufferings. As a punishment for this humane weakness, defeating the ends of justice, the unfortunate official was given the knout, his tongue was cut out, and he was sent to end his days in Siberian banishment.

THE HETMAN PLATOV

IN the days of public rejoicing following the Peace of Paris no hero of the armies of the Grand Coalition which had overthrown Napoleon enjoyed such unrivalled popularity as the Hetman Platov, the leader of the Cossacks of the Don. The versions of his terrifying exploits which became current in Europe were often so exaggerated that the betman – like Mazeppa – began to be considered by a later generation as a character in fiction. Always modest in his own accounts, Platov became the victim of overzealous biographers. It is only in recent years that writers of his own race have succeeded in making clear the history of the stirring events in which be took part and the important military rôle played by the Cossacks during the retreat of the French from Moscow.

During Platov's visit to England in the personal suite of the Emperor Alexander, his fame threatened to eclipse even the reception accorded to the "Tsar Idealist" himself. At a memorable race meeting held in Ascot in the year 1815 the hetman was almost mobbed by his admirers: "his arrival was greeted by a tempest of cheers so prolonged that

they threatened to interrupt the serious business of the occasion. Five men at one time were shaking his hand, each one passing on to a friend the finger that he had enjoyed the honour of holding. An attention even more annoying to the gallant Cossack was offered by a throng of ladies, who, armed with scissors, insisted either upon being presented with locks of the hero's hair, or when, for obvious reasons, this was refused, on cutting souvenirs from the tail of his charger." Yet in spite of this overwhelming reception, Platov always looked back on this stay among the warm-hearted Londoners as the happiest epoch of his life.

Platov was born about the middle of the XVIIIth century at Tcherkass, the old capital of the Don Cossacks.

The exact date of his birth is unknown because in later years he was always careful to conceal his age from his companions-in-arms – many of them younger than his own grandchildren. His military career, like that of the veteran Prince Kutusov, forms a connecting link between the group of brilliant generals who directed the victorious wars of Catherine the Great and the history of the Napoleonic era.

Ivan Platov, the future hetman's father, was a simple Cossack officer who, like his son, was born at Tcherkass. It is considered a noteworthy fact by his biographers that the elder Platov knew how to read and write, advantages which he took pains to secure for his son, young Matvei Ivanovitch. But in the warlike times of Catherine's reign school days were necessarily brief in all Cossack *stanitzi* on the Don. At the age of thirteen we find the future hetman serving as a private in the ranks of the Tcherkask regiment.

Like all true Cossacks Platov welcomed the end of the long peace which was marked by the outbreak of the first Turkish war. Great, therefore, was his disappointment when the elder Platov was summoned (on account of his knowledge of the frontier conditions) to the general staff in Petrograd, so that in his absence his son became charged with the direction of the family's modest affairs. It was in disobedience, therefore, of his father's orders that in 1770 Platov joined his old comrades-in-arms in the Crimea, where they were then serving under the command of the Russian General Dolgorouki. His stay at the main front was, however, not a prolonged one, for we next hear of him stationed among the frontier garrisons of Cossack troops on the shores of the Kouban. With them he engaged in a brisk little campaign against the warlike mountaineers of the Caucasus, a never failing accompaniment of Russia's wars against the Sultan.

During the years 1775-1777 Platov served with the Russian troops engaged in hunting down the rebellious Cossacks of the Jaik, who under their unworthy leader, Pougatchev, were defending their right to follow out their own religious customs and beliefs. After the capture and execution of the *"False Tsar Peter,"* Platov continued to serve in the border garrison along the Kouban, earning distinction and experience in campaigns against the courageous Tcherkess, Lesghians and the other mountain tribesmen of these romantic regions.

The outbreak of Catherine's second war against the Turks was welcomed by Platov as offering an opportunity for more rapid promotion. At the famous siege of Otchakov he found himself promoted to be a colonel of Cossacks, and in 1789 (when his regiment captured the famous Turkish general Gazan Pasha) Potemkin consented to lend him his powerful support, the surest road to further promotion. To please her favourite the empress appointed Platov *"Hetman of all the Cossacks of the Don,"* and to this title was shortly added that of Governor of the province of Ekaterinoslav.

A few months after this event the young hetman's reputation for personal bravery and his continued warlike success caused Catherine to express a wish to meet the "most famous Cossack of her armies." This high compliment, which was conveyed to Platov through his protector, Potemkin, involved a long and tedious journey to Petrograd. At court he was received with favours which might well have turned the course of his career, or even engaged him in a dangerous rivalry with his patron the favourite.

The great Catherine, although by no means in her first youth, had never ceased to show her interest in gallant – and especially in handsome – soldiers. For those who bravely served her she considered no reward too exalted. So pleased was the Empress with the young Cossack's martial yet modest bearing that she even accorded him the honour of personally conducting him through the marvels of the imperial apartments. For nearly a week the Winter Palace hummed with the news of his good fortune. Ambassadors of Great Powers began to concern themselves with a possible change in the imperial "policy" of the day. But age had not made Catherine more constant. Soon tiring of the simple and soldierly manners of her new favourite, an intimation that she would no longer detain him from his military duties ended his brief career as a courtier. We can well imagine with what relief young Platov quitted the stifling atmosphere of the Winter Palace, heavy with scent and intrigue, to breathe once more the pure breezes of the Don steppes.

Yet this interlude in Platov's military career does not seem to have caused him to lose the favour of the powerful Potemkin. In their cynical enjoyment of power, the group of "ministers" surrounding the Empress had little time for jealousy. Under Zoubov, another favourite promoted by Catherine to be *"Hetman of all the Cossack Armies,"* he fought through the

Persian campaign of 1795 and was present at the fall of Baku and Elizabethpol. The cross of the Order of Saint Vladimir and a sword bearing the legend in diamonds "In recognition of Bravery," was the reward of Platov's services at court and in the field.

The death of Catherine the Great brought her son, the Emperor Paul, to the throne. This imperial Hamlet – whose youth was constantly overshadowed by the fate of his father – had always considered his mother in the light of a usurper. Constant brooding over his wrongs and misfortunes had made him in reality little better than a madman. "You must know," he once declared to a foreign ambassador soon after his accession, "that there is no one worth considering in Russia, except the person to whom I am speaking, and then only during the time I am addressing myself to him." But the Emperor Paul had little of the character of Louis XIV except his overwhelming self-conceit. The Tsar hated everyone who had found favour in his mother's eyes. Every plan by which she had raised her adopted country to be the first Power of Europe, even the glorious military traditions of Catherine's reign, were set at naught and revised. Paul's mania for reforming and his passion for copying Prussian models did not even spare the national uniforms of the Russian army, so suitable for the changing climate and conditions of steppe warfare. These were replaced by tight-fitting Prussian military tunics, plaited queues, buckled shoes, gaiters and the awkward beaver hats worn by Frederick's troops of the line.

How seriously the Emperor was attached to these military details is shown by his treatment of the veteran general Souvarov, hero of a hundred victorious battles, who was sent to Siberia for composing a little rhyme in which the virtues of "wigpowder" and "gun-powder" were somewhat disrespectfully compared.

" Russia no longer looks for conquest, nor warlike aggrandizement — only for peace." This was the platitudinous message which Paul's diplomats were instructed to deliver to a distracted Europe!

In pursuit of his mania for undoing the schemes of his great predecessor, the Russian troops on the frontiers of Persia were so abruptly withdrawn that the brave little kingdom of Georgia, which for centuries had formed the bulwark of Christianity against the forces of Islam, was left to bear, almost without warning, the brunt of the uneven struggle.

During this time the subject of our sketch, the Hetman Platov, like many others of Catherine's party, had the misfortune to fall under the morbid displeasure of the Emperor. No reasons were given for the order which exiled him to the provincial capital of Kostroma, from which place he was soon afterwards brought under heavy guard to Petrograd and imprisoned in the fortress of St. Peter and St. Paul.

Platov has himself described the painful conditions of his captivity passed in company with many other distinguished officials of Catherine's reign. How this second involuntary stay in the capital must have recalled strange memories of his first visit! "Even in Summer the dampness and cold which radiate from the walls of our prisons penetrate to the very bones. In the hot season we all suffer from fever. In winter, however, our condition is far worse. We must then huddle together about the stoves to keep from freezing, in spite of the blinding sting of the wood smoke which fills our cells. Nearly all of us are half blind from this cause. Our only distraction is to watch the antics of the rats. These are everywhere, but though at first odious, they have finally became my most sympathetic companions."

Like many another brave soldier of Catherine's army, Platov might have remained forgotten among the sad company gathered in this famous fortress until death released him, had not a fresh turn in the weather-vane of Paul's foreign policy incidentally recalled him to his sovereign's memory. The course of the French Revolution had been diverted by the personal ambitions of Bonaparte into channels more acceptable to Paul's autocratic views. Moreover the cowardice or treachery shown by his Austrian allies during the campaign against the French in Switzerland had cooled his enthusiasm for the Hapsburgs. Napoleon's great victory over the Austrian armies at Marengo was applauded all over Russia. The English ambassador, always alert to note the varying changes of Paul's enthusiasms, now reported that "portraits of Bonaparte are found even in the public rooms of the imperial palaces."

Bonaparte, on the other hand, lost no opportunity to reconcile Paul to the great changes which had taken place since the Revolution on the map of Europe. Soon after an interchange of notes marking beyond a doubt the new disposition of the Russian foreign office, the courts of Europe heard with astonishment of a "great project" upon which the armies of France and Russia were about to embark. From the correspondence which was now exchanged between Paul and Napoleon with respect to an invasion of India it is difficult to determine how deeply Napoleon entered into the practical details of the adventurous scheme. His doubts concerning its successful outcome are everywhere apparent. But as a diversion likely to trouble public opinion in Great Britain, and as a lure whereby the Russian monarch might be more firmly attached to his system, he undoubtedly saw in this venture a useful adjunct of his policies. In documents minutely setting forth the military itinerary which lay before the Franco-Russian troops may still be seen the objections noted down in the handwriting of the greatest general of his age, followed by the "triumphant" refutations of the Russian Emperor scrawled in an unformed schoolboy's hand. According to this plan thirty-five thousand picked French troops (at Paul's request these were to be commanded by General Masséna, the hero of the great Russian disaster at Zurich) were to descend the Danube in vessels requisitioned from the Austrian government. Crossing the Black Sea to Taganrog, flatboats were then to carry them up the course of the river Don to Piati-Isbiankaja. Here it was planned that the expedition should march overland to Tsaritzin on the Volga. Descending that great river to Astrakhan, the French detachment would cross the Caspian to Asterabad, where a corps of 35,000 Russians were to await their arrival.

Impatient to take the first steps in the execution of his "great design," Paul now ordered Russian troops once more to occupy the Caucasus and on the demand of the son of the heroic Tsar Heraclius of Georgia, this warlike little kingdom was peacefully incorporated in the Russian empire. At the same time General Knorring was ordered to lead a Russian division against the upper Indus, passing through the country under the jurisdiction of the powerful Khans of Khiva and Bokhara. To cooperate with this difficult campaign the hetman of the Cossacks of the Don, Orlov Denissov, was ordered to proceed at once to Orenburg.

The soldier who, of all his officers, could best aid the emperor in carrying out the proposed plan, was a forgotten prisoner in the fortress of St. Peter and St. Paul. To transfer the ex-hetman Platov from a prison cell to the command of an important military expedition was an act which presented no incongruities to a convinced autocrat like Paul. The imprisoned Cossack chieftain, thus suddenly drawn from the society of rats and convicts by a summons to the Imperial Council, was confident that his last hour had come. Shaved and dressed in his old-fashioned uniform – scorning the assurances of his jailers – he bade farewell to his comrades, and marched bravely forth to his expected execution. His surprise may be imagined when he found himself suddenly introduced by a side door to the Winter Palace, where, after a meal such as he had not enjoyed for months, he was led directly into the private study of the Emperor.

Reassured by the Emperor's manner (which as Platov himself tells us seemed to ignore both the hetman's past wrongs and Paul's share therein) the prisoner of yesterday was invited to give his opinion upon the intricate military affairs which now engaged the Tsar's attention. On the table before the strangely assorted pair were spread out the only available maps of the almost unknown regions of Asia where Paul had planned to initiate the rôle of Alexander the Great. No one knew better than Platov himself the unsurmountable difficulties of these desert wastes. "Here is the path I have chosen for you – the route of Alexander the Great," said the Emperor dramatically. "Can you follow it, to India?"

Although recognizing at a glance the military faults and incongruities of the scheme proposed by the Emperor Paul, Platov (as he declares in his memoirs) was fully "resolved to follow any line which led away from the prison of St. Peter and St. Paul." Without further committing himself he gravely nodded his approval of everything the imperial strategist had proposed. More than ever satisfied with his own plan and his manner of choosing a general to carry it out, the Emperor dismissed his late prisoner. On the lapel of Platov's coat, stained and discoloured by the smoke and dirt of his prison, glittered the high Russian order of St. John of Jerusalem. In his pocket was a draft on the imperial treasury for an almost unlimited amount, and a snuffbox ornamented with the insignificant features of his master. It is more than probable that Platov, whose breast had already been decorated by the great Catherine "with as many crosses as a graveyard," cared but little for these honours. compared to the liberty he thus so strangely regained. Without waiting the expiration of the three days graciously allowed him in Petrograd, the hetman set out for the Don, where he was received as one returning from the dead. Cutting short all demonstrations of welcome he began at once to gather the troops of the warlike community, without, however, disclosing the objects of the ill-planned campaign upon which they were to set forth. Every Cossack capable of carrying a lance was ordered to report at a given rendezvous, bringing with him two horses and six weeks' provisions. In the month of January, 1801, 27,500 Cossacks of the Don were able to set forth on their long march towards the deserts of Asia.

In Orenburg the Russian governor, Bakmetiev, had assembled provisions, camel transport and even a corps of interpreters speaking the languages or dialects of the numerous tribes whose countries they were to traverse. Before their departure from the fortress a letter from Paul was read promising the Cossacks "all the riches of India." Plunging boldly into the almost trackless wilderness that lay beyond the frontier outposts the Russian troops travelled like mariners across an unknown sea, marching, or rather navigating, by means of the compass and observed positions of the stars.

On the horizon hovered great bands of horsemen, Bashkirs and Kalmoucks, astonished to see a body of troops so numerous that they could not be attacked by any known tactics of desert warfare. Without fear of surprise or ambuscade the troops marched at their ease and in open order. But another danger now threatened the Cossack army. The distant objective of their march having become rumoured about, the Kirghiz camel drivers began deserting with their animals, thus depriving the Russians of the only means of transport. It even became necessary to abandon a large part of the provisions, tents and other equipment necessary for the troops.

Moreover, on account of the intense cold the supply of fuel was rapidly disappearing. The Cossacks, unaccustomed to economy in this respect, insisted upon building roaring fires during the long cold nights. Sickness also broke out in the ranks and the problem of transporting those no longer capable of remaining in the saddle added to Platov's difficulties. In the absence of all recognizable marks in the featureless landscape one day's march appeared to the impatient and half mutinous troops precisely like that of the preceding day. The desert mirage, amazingly vivid in these latitudes, showed them the domes of distant cities and oases which they took to be Khiva or Bokhara, and the next moment dissolved these fairy scenes ito clouds of mist. Such phenomena increased the superstitious fears of the Cossacks. Many declared that the whole army was bewitched by Tartar sorcerers and that they were all marching forward without advancing towards their goal. At last the hetman was obliged to yield to the demands of the mutineers. Glad of an excuse which hindered him from further carrying out plans he considered impossible of execution, he ordered that a camp be formed to rest the tired horses and attend to the sick. At the same time he sent out scouts and patrols in order to obtain news of Knorring's expedition. All soon realized that this halt was but the preliminary to an inevitable return. In the mirage which haunted the desert horizon Platov now began to see once more the slender golden spire which crowns the grim silhouette of the fortress of St. Peter and St. Paul.

It was at this critical juncture that a messenger arrived with the welcome news of the sudden death of the Russian Emperor. Paul had been the victim of a palace revolution which resulted in seating his son, the popular young Grand Duke Alexander, on the throne. All Russia breathed more freely, but nowhere, we may be sure, was the news of this change more welcome than in the famine-stricken camp where, on the pitiless

Turcoman desert, the uncalculating ambition and faulty geography of a tyrant had engaged the Cossacks of the Don in a hopeless quest. Thus ended the first and last attempt of an invasion of India by land, a plan which, since the days of Peter the Great, had tempted the ambition of succeeding Russian sovereigns.

The years that ensued between the events just related and the outbreak of the Napoleonic wars of 1807-1812 were perhaps the happiest of Platov's life. The Russian biographer assures us "the hetman was looked upon by the Don Cossacks as a father to whom the wants of all the Cossacks were as well known as the needs of his own family." The peaceful duties of administrating the Cossack *stanitzi* kept him more busily employed than during his most energetic campaigns. The capital of the Don provinces, Novotcherkask, was moved under his direction to its present site, and the ancient capital, always subject to the inundations of the Don, was abandoned. The foundations of several important public buildings were laid, and among the first of these a cathedral and public schools. The education of the Cossack children was the subject of the hetman's particular attention. A school system was organized caring for the needs of the children in the most remote *stanitzi*. Those who could not otherwise secure the services of a teacher were brought to Novotcherkask at the public expense.

At the same time Platov used all his powerful influence to preserve the traditions of Cossack national life. To those who wished to change the "old frontier ways" he pointed out that it was only their military organization which differentiated the Cossacks from the surrounding peasant population, whose abject condition they all despised. Towards a class of young Cossack officers, who thought by abandoning their characteristic uniforms and by imitating the ways and manners of the local Russian nobility to raise themselves above their fellows, he was especially severe. Recognizing that in universal service – the basis of the Cossack system of land tenure – lay their chief usefulness to the Russian state, he mercilessly enforced the discipline necessary to ensure their privileged position. Even at the present day the lessons taught by the worthy hetman are playing their part in keeping the Cossacks alive to their duties in the great struggle which Russian democracy is waging against Bolshevism and the poison of Marxian Kultur.

At the outbreak of the first Russian campaign against the Emperor Napoleon, in 1807, Platov was nearly sixty years of age. He might, therefore, have honourably asked for permission to continue his calm and useful retirement. But like another famous Cossack leader, Mazeppa, his most renowned exploits were to be performed after the age when a general – and especially a leader of light cavalry – is considered unfit for active service. During the Turkish wars Russia's Cossack cavalry and the peculiar tactics which their officers had perfected had aroused the interest of military students all over Europe. But although invaluable for scouting and reconnoissance, and for harrying the flanks of an enemy or turning defeat into a rout, the Cossacks were nevertheless the despair of the German and Austrian tacticians of the Emperor Alexander's staff. The ideal soldier, according to these experts, was embodied in the little blocks of wood they could manœuvre so convincingly across their field maps.

When, as only too often happened, these theoretical operations refused to repeat themselves as planned, it was the Russian troops, especially the Cossacks, who were generally blamed. But Prince Koutusov, the popular hero of Catherine's wars, who recognized the irreconcilable differences between the Russian and German methods and shared the national "distrust" of Alexander's foreign advisers, placed great reliance upon the Cossack levies. His whole campaign against Napoleon's army after the disaster of Moscow was indeed a strategic development of Cossack principles – the manœuvres which had been practised for centuries upon the broad plain of Scythia since the days of Darius' invasions.

To carry out his plan of a long and orderly retreat – leading his enemy ever deeper into the treacherous steppes – he needed just such mobile troops as were furnished by the soldiers of the Don, the Kouban, the Terek and the Urals. But only a leader enjoying their respect and confidence could turn their military talents to the best account. Platov's personal popularity and prestige made him an invaluable leader of these redoubtable squadrons among whom the free Cossack spirit too often degenerated into license and indiscipline. For this reason, in spite of his advanced years, Koutousov urged him to take part in the coming campaign.

In treating of the glorious campaign of 1812 – the uprising of the entire Russian nation against Napoleon's ambition for World Power – only the part played by the Cossack troops will be considered here. Thirty-six thousand Cossacks formed the vanguard of the heroic army which first advanced against Napoleon. These were divided into fifty *polki* or "regiments," each provided with its own light artillery. The flying column under Platov's immediate command was composed of fourteen regiments, to which were added a few *chasseurs* and dragoons. The principal duty assigned to the Donskoi troops was that of covering the flanks of the second army under the command of his old friend and patron, Prince Bagration.

A great rivalry soon sprang up between Napoleon's scouts – Polish uhlans and hussars – and the Cossack cavalry. During the advance of King Jerome's army (at the very beginning of the French attack) three regiments of uhlans on their way to Novgoroudka were cut off in the village of Karelichi by two regiments of Platov's troops. The greater part of the uhlans fell or were taken prisoner at the first onslaught, while the rest were pursued to the very outpost of Jerome's headquarters.

For more than a month these combats between Polish and Cossack cavalry continued. It was largely due to such minor engagements fought between these old-time enemies that the advance of the main French army was so seriously retarded, a delay which enabled Bagration to retire in good order to his entrenchments at Bobrinsk.

This task accomplished Platov was ordered to cross the Dnieper and to join the first army. While attached to this new command Platov and his Cossacks witnessed the terrible disaster of the first battle of Bordino. While this engagement was not of a character to give the Cossacks an opportunity to employ their peculiar tactics, nevertheless Prince Koutousov, the aged commander-in-chief, declared that Platov was "getting too old for active service." Showing little mercy for an officer who had grown grey in the same service as himself, Koutousov relieved the veteran of his command in the field, ordering him to proceed to the Don in order to gather new reinforcements.

Platov's soldierly rejoinder to this crushing blow was redoubled activity in serving the cause of his beloved country, now grown so desperate. Every Cossack military colony had long since been swept of recruits at the first call to arms. Only the old men and children too young to bear arms had been left to help the women in tilling the field. It was among these veterans of Catherine's wars and their younger grandchildren that Platov determined to find material for his new regiments. Weapons were improvised from the ancient trophies of former Cossack campaigns, taken from the walls and made over to suit more modern munitions. From the Monument of Victory erected after the Turkish wars before the new church in Novotcherkask six ancient bronze cannon were recovered and made serviceable by mounting them on cart wheels. In an incredibly short space of time this heroic "forlorn" was ready for the road. Between grey-headed heroes who had served with Potemkin and Souvarov were placed children of twelve and fourteen glowing with pleasure at this unexpected privilege of playing a soldier's part. None but a Cossack population could have produced such a levy. At their head marched the septuagenarian hetman, now once more serving as the simple colonel of a Cossack *polk*.

The arrival of these recruits in the Russian headquarters camp at Tarantino was the occasion of a spirited ovation. Without regard to the presence of Koutousov, the Cossack sires, in high spirits, showered good-natured abuse upon the regular regiments drawn up at parade. "We have come to rescue you with all our poor little grandchildren," they cried.

Already they had proven their worth. A *sotnia* from one of these veteran regiments (the regiment of Isvolaski) had averaged sixty versts a day in their march from the Don to Tarantino, a record scarcely equalled in Russian military annals. Even the stern Koutousov was moved at the sight of these glorious recruits reporting for duty long before the time set for their arrival. When among the greybeards in their ranks he recognized comrades-at-arms who had served with him in former campaigns, he called Platov from the head of his regiment and fell into his outstretched arms. While the two veterans mingled their tears of joy and reconciliation, fathers, sons and grandchildren toasted each other with boisterous Cossack cheer around the same bivouacs.

The delayed retreat of Napoleon's Grand Army which began soon after the events described now gave the Cossacks their terrible opportunity. During the long stay in Moscow, the French troops had lost all discipline. Against their disordered fleeing host, concerned only with reaching the Russian frontier, the Cossacks were able to drive home their continual, untiring attacks. To assist them in gathering the terrible harvest peasant bands sprang up everywhere. Even these undisciplined partisans and such feeble troops as the veteran levies of the Don could now venture to measure their strength against the most famous regiments of Napoleon's guard. The English "Cossack" Wilson in his memoirs recounts a ghastly saying current in the Cossack ranks, "It is a shame to leave such skinny ghosts wandering about without their graves."

Platov, restored once more to service with his old division, had singled out the corps commanded by the Viceroy of Italy as his special prey, troops which still courageously kept up a semblance of discipline. All day, through the driving snow, the fugitives saw far across the terrifying expanse of white plain about them, a long dark line following their march. Just out of musket shot, bands of Cossacks prowled awaiting nightfall. Around every bivouac their fitful sleep was haunted by a nightmare of Cossack pikes. To fall but a few paces behind the column meant a terrible death at the hands of outraged peasantry and their Cossack protectors.

On October 28, near Rabouga, an attack in force was made by a Cossack flying column, and the long straggling line of fugitives, dragging itself like a wounded snake across the steppes, was cut in two. The rear half, thus hopelessly cut off, tried to save itself by breaking up into little bands. Sixty-four cannon fell into the hands of the Cossacks. The greater part of these troops perished from cold on the steppes or were killed by the Cossacks. When the unfortunate Viceroy had taken refuge at Smolensk (without cavalry or transport and with only twelve cannon), Platov, gathering fifteen regiments and all the Don artillery, next engaged Ney and the heroic rearguard, taking from the "Lion," as even his enemies called the famous marshal, 1300 prisoners and four cannon.

At Kovno, where the enemy were at last driven from Russian soil, Ney and his rearguard made a final heroic stand. After another victory stubbornly won, Platov and his Cossacks heard a Te Deum in the public square, the horsemen drawn up in grim and silent ranks, while the inhabitants knelt about them. Before the bells which rang out so joyfully in the cold air had ceased their pealing, the Cossacks swept beyond the frontier into "Europe."

History next notices Platov and his Cossacks preparing to take part in the attack on Danzig, still in the possession of Napoleon's German allies. The news that Frederick William of Prussia had finally summoned up courage to join the Alliance in the "*Befreiungskrieg*" caused the surrender of that place. On the road near Kalice, Platov was sent to meet the none too heroic Hohenzollern and soon after conducted him to the General Staff of Emperor Alexander, the real Liberator of Germany. At the famous "Battle of the Nations," fought at Leipzig in October, 1813, Platov received the Cross of St. Andrew.

To reward his conduct during the engagement near Frankfort-on-Oder, there remained no higher honour to bestow upon the hetman. The thanks of his sovereign and a diamond aigrette to ornament his Cossack *Tshapka* were the only official means of recognizing the valor of his troops. It was, perhaps, fortunate that the war was drawing to a close!

The last warlike enterprise in which we hear of Platov and his Cossacks was their chivalrous attempt to rescue the captive Pope at Fontainebleau. But the unfortunate head of the Roman Church (dragged about together with the royal treasures of France in the wake of the fallen conqueror) had already left that place. Thus the strangest booty that could have fallen into the bands of the orthodox Cossacks of the Don escaped their well- meant efforts.

Soon after the peace of Paris, Platov made his famous visit to London of which we have already had occasion to speak. The "hundred days" following Napoleon's return from the island of Elba cost the veteran a last long ride across Europe to the battle of Waterloo.

His next return to the now peaceful shores of the Don was, however, to be the last. For three years the tired veteran enjoyed unbroken rest and the inevitable reaction ensued. The steel springs of his energy uncoiled, and after a short illness due to a cold the Hetman Platov died peacefully in his bed in the year 1818.

THE COSSACKS OF TO-DAY: ORGANIZATION AND GOVERNMENT

AT the close of the imperial régime, the term "Cossack" was legally applied to a distinct class or caste within the Russian state, differentiated by well-defined rights and duties from the ordinary subjects of the empire. For military reasons the Tsar's government fostered the clan spirit and *esprit de corps* which has always characterized the "Free People."

To the North Russian peasant the Cossack troops were often associated with measures of police and oppression. Historical reasons, as we have seen, have also played their part in separating the Cossack from the *Moujik* class – whose infinite docility the former have always regarded with contempt and aversion. Yet the distrust existing between them and the "great gray mass" of the Russian peasantry did not prevent the Cossacks from playing a notable rôle in the events which brought about the constructive revolution of 1917.

The Cossacks are at present organized into eleven "armies," each occupying its own settlement or allotted territory. Their *stanitzi*, or settlements, are generally distributed along the frontiers, old and new, of what was formerly the Empire of All the Russias. Officially these *stanitzi* were known as the territories of the Cossack armies of the Don, Ural, Terek, Kuban, Orenburg, Astrakhan, Trans-Baikal, Siberian, Siemriechinskoe (Seven Rivers), Amur and Ussuri. (*See* Map.) Thus with every Cossack "army" or its subdivision was associated some definite grant of land to which it was "territorially" attached.

The Cossacks of the later "armies," formed for the purpose of patrolling and safeguarding the long frontiers of Russia's newly acquired Asiatic provinces, never enjoyed the same generous grants of land that were conferred upon the earlier subdivisions, such as the Cossacks of the Kouban and Terek.

On the other hand, the present territories of the Cossacks of the Don and Uralsk represent but a small portion of the huge "Free Steppes" over which their ancestors established their control. Indeed, the vague boundaries of these holdings were only "confirmed" when the advance of non-Cossack pioneers made such an act necessary. The policy vigorously maintained by the imperial government was that of granting land in the neighbourhood of Cossack outposts only in return for military service. The system adopted – even during the closing years of the empire – did not differ materially from that employed by the early Tsars. Moreover, in order to foster the community spirit, all land ceded by the Russian crown to the different Cossack "armies" was to be held rigorously in common. This principle with certain modifications brought about by the passing of the "frontier conditions" (notably in the Don region) underlies the system of Cossack land tenure to the present day. Each adult male Cossack "soul" is entitled to the use of 30 dessiatines (about 75 acres) of agricultural land. These allotments may be re-distributed yearly, and the quantity increased, if local conditions (such as the quality of the land) make such a step desirable. The areas set aside for "military purposes" are used for forestry, and horsebreeding, and as a reserve for the future needs of the community.

Under the former imperial régime, the administration of the Cossack "armies" was placed directly under the ministry of war, where a special "Chancellery" had charge of all matters affecting this class of citizens. A special "Committee of the Cossack armies" aided the Chancellery in its decisions, and all questions both of civil and military character were decided by these two organizations. While in theory elective, the members of this advisory committee were formerly in reality appointed by the Minister of War. One of the first acts of the various Cossack congresses which ratified the change to a republican form of government was to provide for a popular and representative membership of this important body. The principal Cossack armies, viz.: Don, Uralsk, Terek, Kouban, Orenburg and Astrakhan, have each one permanent representative on this committee, while the smaller Cossack communities of Western and Eastern Siberia have each one delegate.

The head of each "army" preserves the ancient title of *ataman*, an office usually uniting the military and civil duties of a governor-general. At the head of each *stanitza* — which usually comprises from one to four villages according to the size of their population — is placed a *stanitzi ataman*, who is responsible for the general order. Out of respect for Cossack particularism, each *stanitza* in theory became an administrative unit enjoying the fullest autonomy.

The actual government in most of these communities is generally exercised by a council of Cossack elders, generally men past military age, whose patriarchal decisions are respected by all. This council or *sbor* is responsible to a *stanitza* gathering in which all the Cossack heads of families are represented. In view, however, of the increasing population and the unwieldy proportions which these gatherings attained in many of the larger *stanitzi* the old principle of the *obshi kroug*, i.e., the "Circle of All," is generally limited to communities not exceeding twenty or thirty families. In the larger communities a representative system has been adopted based on the universal suffrage of men over twenty-five years of age. Decisions must be reached in all important affairs by the vote of at least a two-thirds majority.

In the Cossack *stanitzi* non-Cossacks, or "persons not of the military class," are permitted to live on the payment of certain dues to the community, but without the right to vote or hold office. (Jews were formerly rigorously excluded from the enjoyment of this privilege.)

Cossacks have the same fondness for cattle raising and other pastoral pursuits noticeable in the inhabitants of nearly all new countries. Like the true "cowboy" of the Far West – with whom he has much in common – the Cossack will only put his hand to the plow when driven to it by the sternest necessity. Although in many parts of the Cossack country the soil of the steppes is surpassingly rich, the rigours of a continental climate are felt with especial severity. In these vast almost treeless plains droughts, floods and other climatic extremes are enemies of the Cossack husbandmen.

Under the imperial government the breeding of horses and cattle was especially encouraged in order to furnish mounts for the cavalry, and to ensure the best results the Ministry of Agriculture provided the Cossack herders with blooded stock. Breeding farms are established for the direction and supervision of this industry at convenient points.

Besides horses a great part of the wealth of the Cossack nations consists in their herds of cattle, sheep, swine, and camels. Indeed in many parts of the *stanitzi* the size of these herds forms the chief criterion of Cossack wealth and position, much in the same way that this standard is applied among nomad races.

The old tradition that pictures the Cossack troops as a levy of wild horsemen, only useful for the purpose of partisan warfare, in no way represents the actual state of their military capabilities. Besides living from childhood in a military atmosphere their officers are drilled with especial severity for their long period of duty. Under the old régime, while special military institutions existed for Cossack officers, they were subjected to the same educational requirements as the cadets graduating from regular military schools. Moreover, no amount of training could take the place of the marvellous *esprit de corps* – an almost instinctive "clan" feeling – existing in every Cossack regiment.

The introduction of universal military service in 1874, and the enactment of laws by which every male Russian was called upon to take up his share in the burden of state defence, removed many of the differences existing between the Cossacks and their peasant or *moujik* neighbours. But in spite of the important change thus realized the military traditions of the Cossack race remained unchanged and the imperial government continued to treat them as a distinct body in the community. Each Cossack was still required to furnish his own horse, uniform and weapons, and the only changes made in the old conditions of Cossack service had in view placing the Cossack armies in a position enabling them to co-operate with the regular troops of the Russian line.

Nearly all the Cossack troops engaged in the heroic struggle which the Russian army made on the side of the Allies during the opening years of the World War, were cavalry formations. The levy of the united Cossack armies just before the war constituted a minimum of 144 cavalry regiments, 830 *sotnia* or "hundreds" and a quota of light Cossack artillery, accompanying the infantry divisions. As Cossack cavalry drill included a certain training in infantry tactics, their services were useful even in trench warfare, but it was as scouts and raiders that the traditional Cossack qualities gained for these troops such well-deserved reputation.

For military purposes all male Cossacks are divided into two general categories, active and reserve. The active category is again divided into three divisions:1. Preparatory, composed of Cossacks and cadets undergoing military instruction.2. Line Cossacks.3. Depot or reserve for the second division.

Cossack military service begins at eighteen years and is continued as follows: three years in the preparatory class; twelve years in the line; five years in the reserve. The "line" category, in view of the long service required, is divided into three divisions, only the first of which serves constantly with the colours, while the other two are allowed to remain near their homes subject to "the call to arms." (See *Russian Encyclopedia*, article by A. Saroff.)

With the negligible exception of twenty infantry "hundreds" and a greatly reduced quota of light Cossack artillery, nearly all the Cossack troops serve as cavalry, or "dismounted cavalry."

In addition to the regular Cossack troops the imperial armies included a division of cavalry, armed and drilled according to Cossack methods, but exclusively recruited among the war-like tribes of the Tcherkess, Abkbazes, Lesghians, Daghestani, etc. These'wild horsemen, who compose the celebrated "Dikki Division" or "Wild Division," enjoy not only a great reputation for reckless bravery but also for the excesses which they are reputed to commit in enemy territory. Few, if any, of these troops are Cossacks, and only the similarity of dress and equipment causes them to be confused with the latter. On the other band a bitter rivalry exists between them and the true Cossack troops against whom their ancestors were so long engaged in frontier feuds and skirmishes. (This is the division which General Kornilov was reported to be leading in his much misunderstood movement against the former Provisional Government.)

The Cossack divisions preserved their discipline to the last during the terrible moments when Bolshevik propaganda was successfully sowing disorder in the Russian lines. As noted elsewhere, the Cossack regiments everywhere gave their support to the changes brought about by the constructive revolution of March 1917 (conducted along lines so acceptable to the traditions of the "Free People"). By keeping intact military organization most of the Cossack regiments were able then to reach their own territory during the horrors of the Bolshevik demobilization. They thus escaped the lot of so many wretched peasant soldiers of the old régime, who found it necessary to enlist in the ragged regiments of the Red Guards in order to keep body and soul together. When the Bolshevik directorate, which had replaced the officialdom of the old régime at Petrograd, sought to obtain Cossack support, they found the Cossack territories organized, not only to conduct their own affairs, but also to resist dictation from without.

It is perhaps premature to consider here the problem of the place which the Cossacks will occupy in relation to the rest of "What was Russia." When the ominous symbol of the red flag everywhere replaced the national standard throughout Northern Russia – through the teachings of materialistic Socialist doctrines – "class consciousness" took the place of patriotic ideals. The blue and yellow flag of the old Cossack Ukraine immediately appeared in the south, an unmistakable answer to these denationalizing influences. The ideal maintained in all the Cossack territories is that of a Russian federal republic, wherein a large measure of autonomy will be allowed the widely differing peoples and districts who were "gathered together" by the long imperialistic process of the old régime. The opposition of the Bolsheviki at Petrograd to this logical desire for decentralization, and the eagerness with which Lenine and his associates seized upon the machinery and methods of Tsardom for their own form of "government," will probably for some time form an obstacle to any close union between north and south. Here again, however, geographical factors, notably the absence of any natural frontiers separating the older provinces of "Muscovy" from "New Russia," will be a force making for future reunion. At a time when Russia is distracted by the attempts of doctrinaires to solve the vast problems of land tenure left by the collapse of the imperial regime, it is interesting to consider the present situation of the Cossack land holder. The *stanitzi* represent a system of communal ownership developed by practical experience and adjustment through a long period of time, and thoroughly adapted to the needs of the Cossack community. Unlike the grinding tyranny of the *mir* – the primitive communal system under which the Russian peasants of the north sought to administer their own affairs – the Cossack system has been able to give wide latitude to individual effort, and even to adapt itself to the passing of frontier conditions by frankly admitting the right to private ownership. Thus land (such as orchard and homestead land) where permanent improvements have been made through the owner's own outlay of work or capital becomes, with certain restrictions, private property. It is, therefore, easy to understand why Bolshevik propaganda has met with so little success, not only among the peasant proprietors of the Ukraine, where Cossack civilization ceased to exist many years ago, but also in the newer Cossack territories, of the "armies" established during the last century along the eastern frontiers of New Russia. In spite of the infiltration of landless peasants from the North among the Cossack settlements, the doctrines of Marxian Socialism have generally met with a hostile reception throughout the Cossack territories.

The situation was well set forth in the homely language of a delegate of the Uralsk Cossacks to the Cossack congress in Petrograd: "The Cossacks – or 'Free People' – of Russia have not maintained their liberty and manhood during these centuries of crushing autocratic tyranny without learning how to preserve their own liberties in their own fashion. The spectacle afforded us by the prophets of a Socialistic cult imported from Germany and preached by an alien race is enough to disgust any lover of freedom, to whatever nation he may belong. It seems to be forgotten in certain parts of Russia that in the organization and administration of our *kasak* lands we have ourselves developed what may be called the only practical system of community life to be found in actual operation anywhere on the world's surface.

"We, therefore, demand, and feel ourselves more than ever prepared to insist upon, the maintenance under a democratic order of the privilege to manage our own affairs – a privilege which could not be withheld from us under a tyrannical autocracy. This can only be secured, we feel certain, through a régime of complete local autonomy embracing all the widely differing provinces of the old empire. The geographical character of the Russian empire clearly indicates what form of government should there exist. This should be similar to that prevailing in the United States: a federal republic, wherein the Cossack territories, our old neighbours of the Ukraine and the regions of North Russia, will all find their place, and freedom to live their own lives according to their own traditions and aspirations."

HISTORY OF THE COSSACKS

THE COSSACKS OF TO-DAY: THE DON

ONE might seek in vain to-day in many parts of the old Cossack Ukraine for traces of its former masters. Although a modern statue of Bogdan Hmelnicky stands in the public square of Kiev, the Cossack element of the old border capital may be said to have almost disappeared. Yet throughout all the vast territory of South Russia, the traditions of the days of Cossack ascendency are still a precious heritage. The descendants of the Freemen inscribed on the old military registers, and the "little proprietor" or *obnodvortzi* of Kharkov and Poltava, feels himself the equal of the former great landlords of Northern Russia. Even the none too reputable memories of the "heroes" of the later *sitch* — the license and disorderly existence of the Zaporogian Brotherhood — are proudly recalled on account of the devotion to the principles of personal liberty which kept alive the spark of free manhood in the face of a Russia sunk in serfdom.

Although the plains of the Ukraine about Kiev and Kharkov have long since been abandoned by the "Free People" — and the wild riders of the steppes have disappeared in a cloud of dust and a scamper of hoofs towards the more congenial frontiers of Asiatic Russia — their spirit remains alive in the individualistic and independent peasant landholders of

Little Russia.

Any description of the "old Cossack" country of South Russia, notably the provinces of the Don, must first take into account the geographical influences of the great steppes upon the development of this typical civilization.

The great prairies of wild grass have given way to far-stretching wheat fields, and the Cossack *stanitzi* have been replaced by the villages of South Russian peasants. Nevertheless conditions peculiar to the Black Sea littoral still give a characteristic note to the scenery. Travellers of every race and country have exhausted their vocabulary in trying to convey some idea of the effect made upon the observer by the ceaseless uniformity of this landscape. The reader will, therefore, be spared a repetition of these descriptions and asked instead to consider the more cheerful side of the subject – the enormous agricultural possibilities and the stores of natural wealth which in many places underlie these plains.

For in spite of their monotony when viewed from the standpoint of scenery the steppes of Little Russia are perhaps the richest agricultural region in the world. Their fertility is due to the famous *tsherno zemli* or "black earth" which covers the underlying strata for more than a yard in thickness – a deposit which except for certain sandy stretches, extends over nearly the entire southern portion of Russia from the Dnieper to the Caspian. In many places the name popularly given this rich soil is no exaggeration, for when newly turned by the plow it is almost as black as coal. The composition of this natural garden soil is due to a century- long process. Layers of decaying vegetation are deposited by the natural crop of grasses with which these plains are covered every season when left uncultivated. The Russian peasant firmly believes that even without manure or artificial fertilizer the richness of this land is inexhaustible. In many parts scientific investigation seems to bear out his contention that manures are not only superfluous, but detrimental. By plowing to a depth of only six inches the black earth is capable of giving phenomenal crops for five or six years in succession after which if allowed to lie fallow during a few seasons all its fertility appears to return.

It is this natural richness of soil which has brought about the dangerously improvident forms of agriculture to which the Cossack farmer is wedded. Indeed, his inability to compete with more- skillful farmers from less fertile localities lies at the bottom of his slow expropriation by the latter whenever they meet in open competition. If fertility were the only question to be considered in the black earth region, the plains of South Russia would be an agricultural paradise and the Cossacks and peasants inhabiting them the happiest of men. Unfortunately, however, these vast plains are the scene of such sudden and violent changes of weather that no human ingenuity may forestall their effect. So powerful are the rays of the southern sun that disastrous droughts frequently result from a seasonable rainfall deferred but for a few days. Again, under normal winter conditions these plains are covered by snow for five months of the year, forming a necessary protection against the biting frost which otherwise destroys the autumn sowing. But in many parts of the "black earth" region (notably towards the east) the violent winds of winter blow unchecked by hill or forest, carrying away the snowy covering, thereby allowing the soil to freeze sometimes to a depth of a yard or more. In such cases the whole process of sowing must be begun over again in the spring. The preference of the Cossack "old-timer" for cattle raising and breeding, even on such fertile pasturage, is therefore readily to be understood.

In the face of great natural forces wholly beyond his control, fatalism and faith in the omnipotence of a higher power are outstanding characteristics of the Cossack farmer. These qualities carried beyond a certain point are, however, curiously liable to resemble indolence and improvidence. Moreover, these faults are especially dangerous when they do not carry with them the inevitable punishment meted out to men of northern climes. The recent development of the coal and iron fields underlying the agricultural riches of South Russia have done much to change the character of the country and its inhabitants.

The journey from Kiev to Kharkov lies through a classic land of old Cossack history and romance. Yet there is little to remind one of this vanished civilization until the shores of the Don are reached. The contrast between Kiev – its pious silhouette of domes and convent towers rising from the plains of the Dnieper – and Kharkov, the commercial and industrial center of South Russia, is wholly significant of the changes which have overtaken all the western Cossack steppes. Once a mere Cossack settlement, Kharkov lies at the apex of the triangle formed by the great industrial region of South Russia, the Krivoi-Rog. Thus, the iron fields to the north of the Dnieper and the relatively new industrial enterprises of the Donetz coal basin are at its doors. Here center the three essential elements of a modern commercial and industrial El Dorado, i.e., coal, iron and population.

The country in which these rich deposits are found, instead of presenting the barren and unattractive landscape so often associated with mining districts, is covered with wheat-fields and pasture lands. Here it is no uncommon spectacle to see great factories and work shops trailing their plumes of black bituminous smoke across acres of ripening grain – cultivation of which ends only at the foot of their dingy walls.

No wonder that an unconquerable optimism – the true American "western spirit" – pervades the population of these favoured lands. In the clear air and flooding sunlight of the old steppes the northern Russian peasant nature expands with renewed activity. The strong force of "passive resistance," so characteristic of the fatalistic North-Slav civilization, is transformed into a source of boundless physical energy. Even the great workshops and foundries set down among the smiling landscape of fields and orchards lose much of the grim enslaving aspect which characterize the roaring mills of the commercial quarters of Petrograd and Moscow. In the promised land of the old Cossack "Republic of the Don" a new commercial proletariat is arising – a new race of workers who seem to have absorbed some of the sturdy traditions of freedom of the early inhabitants.

Kharkov is a city of about 200,000 inhabitants. The ancient architectural features of the old Ukranian capital have all but disappeared. German influence is evident on every band. A hideous Lutheran Church of raw red brick raises its towers next to the bulbous cupolas of the Russian cathedral, while long streets are lined with houses and shops in the "modern style" of Munich and Carlsruhe. Indeed, the threat of German commercial domination was the direct cause of the early revolutionary movements which broke out in Kharkov in 1917. Another reason for this hostile attitude to the German influence at Petrograd lay in the fact that Kharkov had a large population of Poles from German Poland, who had settled here in the freer commercial atmosphere of Russia.

A few hours ride beyond Kharkov brings the traveller to the first *stanitzi* of the Don Cossacks. The first view of these villages shows them to belong to a different civilization. Comparison with the settlements of the *moujik* workmen who have invaded their territory since the opening of the great modern factories of the Donetz makes this contrast the more remarkable. For the *moujik*, even in new surroundings, long remains true to type.

Even where there is little to prevent their villages from spreading at their ease across the steppes, atavism, or love of each other's company, keeps them crowded about the great red-brick factory buildings, in much the same way that their ancestors huddled about the fortresses of their overlords in the Tartar-raided pinewoods of the north.

The villages inhabited by the true natives of the soil present a far different appearance. The first view of the Cossack *stanitza* shows that their inhabitants take interest not only in the outer appearances, but also concerning questions of cleanliness and sanitation. Another significant fact: schoolhouses begin to appear beside the churches. Each neat fenced garden is of precisely the dimensions prescribed by its owner's military rank in the Cossack *polk*. Even the favourite sunflowers of Little Russia, which stand sentinel about every modest doorway, seem to have been manœuvred into place at the drillmaster's command.

Orchards whose boughs are nearly breaking with their weight of fruit, and an occasional vineyard producing the heady Cossack wine, show the suitability of this rich steppe land for any kind of agriculture. There is, however, another side to the picture. Often for miles at a stretch, the land lies fallow or is left in luxurious pasture for herds of cattle, sheep and sturdy little Cossack horses, among whom occasionally appears the gaunt apocalyptic silhouette of a camel mother and her ungainly offspring. Now and again the sight of a wheat-field stretching in its broad shimmering expanse to a misty horizon gives an insight into the true agricultural possibilities of the Don country, but this latter method of farming "wholesale," reminding one of America or the Canadian provinces of the

West, is in no way indigenous to the soil. Even the implements used in this form of husbandry are American, or the cheaper and flimsier German imitation of American models. Cossack capital is often interested in the development of these grain-lands, yet even the well-to-do Cossack proprietor still infinitely prefers to do his farming by hand. The owner of many such broad acres is more likely to be found hoeing the garden before his own door, or, better still, if his wealth permits, he likes to ride about among his patriarchal flocks and herds. The exploitation of his steppe heritage he leaves to the more mechanically minded farmer of an alien race. Thus the richest profits of the "black earth" belt are garnered by North Russian *moujiks*, or even Tartars or Armenians, rather than by the native *Donskoi*.

An adjustment of relations between the Cossack proprietors and the non-Cossack emigrants now tilling the vast tracts of fertile territory owned in common by the "armies" is one of the most important problems that the future has in store. Whether the land-hungry peasants, who are the lessees of so much of the best Cossack agricultural land, will, with the spread of modern ideas, consent to remain in the relation of tenants towards the community appears highly doubtful.

In the past the rich "black earth" region of the Don and the great coalfields which underlie the old "free steppes" of the Donetz were a greater menace to Cossack institutions than all the attempts of the Russian Tsars to curtail their liberties. The general distaste for trade and industry characterizing the Cossack of the classical days is shared by his descendants. Nearly all mercantile enterprises in the larger towns are in the hands of "strangers." Already a foreign merchant class is growing up among the *stanitzi* under the present policy of toleration. Armenians and Jews are obtaining control of nearly all the retail business in the neighbourhood of

Rostov, and even in the last stronghold of Cossack conservatism – Novotcherkask. Yet, in spite of these signs of the changing times the Cossack still remains to a surprising degree the master in his own house.

The old Cossack communal system, while frequently modified by alien changes, has, in point of fact, prospered exceedingly through this peaceful invasion. A definite share in the increment earned falls to nearly every member of the *stanitza*. Thanks to the conservative workings of Russian law the proprietor is as hard to expropriate as the traditional limpet. This many a promoter of modern, if dubious, prosperity discovered to his cost. With respect to every new project proposed the Cossack officials and elders must have their say, and a spirit of healthy conservatism prevails in their councils.

Even the first glimpse of Novotcherkask, the Cossack capital, will show that here, at least, the old ways are still followed. The streets, though wide and tree-bordered, are often so steep that only a horseman may safely negotiate the grade. On the crest of the highest hill rises the cathedral, a warlike little shrine set about with cannon and other trophies captured from the Turks and English during the Crimean war. In a narrow space of flat ground in front of the *sbor* stands a fine statue of the famous hetman Yermak, the embodiment of Cossack genius, who first conquered Siberia for the Russian empire in the days of Ivan the Terrible. All about the Cathedral are built the great barracks and other military dependencies, while even the private houses clearly indicate the military rank rather than the wealth of their owners.

The little museum, which stands near by, is a veritable Acropolis for the whole *Donskoi* race and the treasures it contains are proudly exhibited to the rare visitor: crudely carved Scythian idols are reminders of the primitive Lords of the Steppes, beautifully chiselled Greek coffins tell of the early commercial colonies established on the Black Sea littoral; marble slabs bearing long inscriptions in Latin record a succeeding influence – that of the Genoese merchant-lords who formerly occupied strategic points on the great *"Highway of the Nations."*

Next to these remains, showing the commercial importance of the Don basin in ancient times, are piously preserved the regalia, half-Tartar, half- Christian, of the old Cossack chieftains and *atamans* of the Don: horsetail standards, copied from those carried before the Asiatic *khans* when they went to war; the heavy silver-gilt *boundchouks*, or war-clubs, formerly the insignia of office, carried by the hetman; *icons* and Cossack standards embroidered with the pictures of wonder-working saints and martyrs of the Ukraine, who accompanied the wild chivalry of the Don in their wars against the Tartars.

There is also preserved in the museum a memento of Empress Cathexine's famous journey through the newly conquered provinces of Southern Russia. It was from the window of a travelling vehicle (which she presented to the *Donskoi*) that she gazed upon the carnivalesque villages which the zeal of her favourite Potemkin caused to be erected all along the route followed by the imperial cortège in its journey across the empty Cossack steppes. The boisterous welcome of the Cossack *stanitzi* of the Don – a contrast to the theatrical rejoicings of the fictitious peasants and *bayaderes* of Potemkin's improvised population – seems to have pleased the august sovereign, who showed them the most gracious side of her character. The *Donskoi*, in turn, elected her an "honorary Cossack" and still cherish the memory of "Mother Catherine's" visit to their capital.

In the library of the museum are carefully preserved the charters and other documents attesting the privileges conferred upon the *Donskoi* race by succeeding Tsars, each confirming the "rights" which the valour of the Cossack armies obtained at the hands of the Russian autocrats.

Novotcherkask is the centre of the Cossack educational system. It boasts of a large institution, the "Academy," whose faculty was famous all over Russia for the sturdy independence of its teachings. The Cossack school system was liberally endowed and illiteracy is lower in the Don *stanitzi* than in any province of the old empire.

THE FRONTIERS OF EUROPE

LESS than a century ago no traveller would have dreamed of crossing the river Don without a strong escort of Russian troops – unless journeying as the guest of some Cossack chieftain or hetman of the "Cossacks of the Black Sea." Concerning this wild country the Englishman Clarke wrote in his celebrated "Travels in the Ukraine" as follows: "Here one finds the Cossack race still living according to the manners and customs of their ancestors. A savage pride in their complete independence is reflected in their dress and manner of existence. Each Cossack is the equal of every other member of the community, whether clad in simple sheep-skins and dwelling in a cave, or inhabiting a fine well-built house and dressed in velvet covered with gold and silver lace." And until the coming of the great trunk line connecting the "Petroleum-Metropolis" of Bakou on the Casplan Sea with Rostov-on-Don, these primitive frontier conditions were to be found existing over all the fertile steppes to the north of the Caucasus. These low-lying plains – the watershed of the Kuban and Terek – were formerly the bed of a great sea or strait connecting the Caspian with the Black Sea. Overlying a sandy substratum filled with the débris of shells and marine life is spread a generous layer of the famous agricultural soil known as "the black earth," the foundation of the agricultural empire of

South Russia. The burial mounds of forgotten, races, huge Kourgans, sometimes still surmounted by rudely carved guardian deities of stone, alone break the flat horizon. These are relics of the Scythian tribes who formerly pastured their flocks on the rich grass that covered these plains. Their numbers show that a numerous population, even in pre-historic times, occupied this favored territory.

About the growing modern city of Ekaterinodar, or "Catherine's gift" – another reminder of the famous visit which that great Russian ruler made to her Cossack territories in South Russia – lies the province where the famous Zaporogian Cossacks were formerly granted lands in order to protect the new frontiers from the inroads of the Tcherkess (Circassians) and other wild mountain tribes of the Caucasus. No encouragement was given these emigrants from the shores of the Dnieper to resume the peculiar organization of their sitch, the armed camp or stronghold whence they formerly set at defiance not only the authority of the Turks and Tartars, but also (when it so pleased their humour) the commands of the Russian Tsars as well. At the present day the descendants of the "Free Companions" differ little from other Cossack communities of the Russian frontier. The enterprise and energy which characterized their forbears is now exercised along wholly peaceful lines.

Foreign agricultural machines are sold in all the principal shops of Ekaterinodar. The spectacle afforded by a bewhiskered Cossack armed with the inevitable dagger, peacefully bestriding an American mowing machine – is wholly typical of the "new days." Bee culture, a traditional occupation of the steppes, where the wildflowers give honey of especially agreeable flavour, is another vocation carried on with success by these descendants of the redoubtable pirates of the Lower Dnieper. In the sandier parts of the plains cattle and sheep raising (pastoral pursuits in which the Cossack population excel) are the principal source of the wealth of these fortunate "Cossacks of the Kuban."

*

Along the foothills of the great Caucasian walls, where the Terek flows through flat, sandy plains to the Caspian Sea, lies the territory of the "Cossack Army of the Terek." To the north lies a salt desert inhabited only by nomad Buddhist Kalmoucks – so isolated by their inhospitable surroundings that they are able to continue the primitive existence of their forefathers within a few hundred versts – as the crow flies – of Russian civilization. These are generally peaceably disposed, but in the mountains to the south of the Terek in the highland fastness of Kabardia and Daghestan dwell Mussulman tribes whose independent spirit is a continual source of petty disorder. Here, in a veritable natural fortress, the Caucasian hero Schamyl and his followers made their last heroic stand against the Russian forces but half a century ago.

In the isolated valleys, unvisited except by that unwelcome fellow brigand, the Russian tax-gatherer, Schamyl's descendants have maintained their tribal customs to the present day. On these the Cossack stanitzi still keep careful watch, for now and again some local Robin Hood ventures to exercise the old tribal right to exact an involuntary toll on the Russian post roads.

In Tolstoi's splendid story, "The Cossack," is found the following description from the Russian view-point of the old Grebenski *stanitzi*, of whom the present-day Cossacks of the Kuban and Terek are the successors: accompanied by his weeping relations and the tribesmen who refused to abandon their feudal chief, even in death. These had become voluntary captives upon hearing the news of his untimely end.

"The whole line of the Terek along which, for some eighty versts, are scattered the stanitzi, or villages of the Grebensky Cossacks, has a distinctive character, by reason not only of its situation, but also of population. The river Terek, which separates the Cossacks from the mountaineers, flows turbid and swift, but still in a broad and tranquil current, constantly depositing gray silt on the low, reed-grown right bank, and undermining the steep but not lofty left bank, with its tangled roots of century-old oaks, decaying plane trees, and underbrush. On the right bank lie auls, or native villages, peaceable but restless; along the left bank, half a verst from the river, and seven or eight versts apart, stretch the Cossack villages. In former times, the majority of these villages or outposts were on the very edge of the river; but the Terek each year, sweeping farther away from the mountains toward the north, has kept undermining them, and now there remain in sight only the old ruins, gardens, pear trees, poplars, and limes, thickly overgrown, and twined about with blackberries and wild grape-vines. No one any longer lives there, and the only signs of life are the tracks on the sand, made by deer, wolves, hares, and pheasants, which haunt such places. A road runs from stanitza to stanitza, through the forest, as a cannon-shot would fly. Along the road are the military stations or cordons, guarded by Cossacks. Between the cordons are watch-towers with sentinels. Only a narrow strip of fertile forest land — say twenty-one hundred feet wide — constitutes the Cossacks' domain. On the north begin the sandy dunes of the Nogai, or Mozdok steppe, stretching far away, and commingling, God knows where, with the Trukhmensky, Astrakhan, and Kirgiz-Kaisak steppes. On the south, beyond the Terek, is the Great Chechnya, the ridge of the Kotchkalosof range, the Black Mountains, then still another sierra, and finally the Snowy Mountains, which are visible, indeed, but which have never yet been trodden by the foot of man. On the fertile strip of forest land, rich in all kinds of vegetation, have lived, since immemorial times, a warlike, handsome, and wealthy, Russian population, professing the "Old Faith," and called the Grebensky Kazaki or Border Cossacks.

Very, very long ago, their ancestors, the Starovyerni, or "Old Believers," fled from Russia and settled beyond the Terek among the Chechens on the ridge – "Greben" – or first spur of the wooded range of the Great Chechnya. These Cossacks intermarried with their new neighbours, the Chechens, and adopted the habits, mode of life, and manners of the mountaineers; but they succeeded in maintaining even there the Russian language and the old belief in their pristine purity. A tradition, still preserved among these Cossacks, declares that the Tsar Ivan the Terrible came to the Terek, invited the elders of the Cossacks from the Ridge to meet him, gave them the land on that side of the river, charged them to live in peace, and promised not to compel them either to subjection or to a change of belief.

From that time to this the Cossack families have kept up their relations with the mountaineers, and the chief traits of their character are love of liberty, laziness, brigandage, and war. The influence of Russia has been exerted only in a detrimental way, by forced conscriptions, the removal of their bells, and the presence of troops quartered among them. The Cossack is inclined to have less detestation for the mountaineer-jigit who has killed his brother than for the soldier who is quartered on him for the sake of protecting his village, but who scents up his hut with tobacco-smoke. He respects his moutain enemy; but he disdains the soldier, whom he regards as an alien oppressor.

In the eyes of the Cossack the Russian peasant is a nondescript creature, uncouth and beneath contempt, the type of which he finds in the peripatetic Little Russian peddler or emigrant, called by the Cossacks shapoval, or tile-wearer.

The height of style there is to dress like the Teberkess. His best weapons are procured from the mountaineers; from them also his best horses are bought or stolen. The young Cossack brave prides himself on his knowledge of the Tartar language, and, when he is on a drunken spree, he speaks Tartar even with his brother.

In fact this petty population of Christians, barricaded in a little corner of the world, surrounded by semi-civilized Mohammedan tribes and by soldiers, regards itself as having attained the highest degree of culture, looks on the Cossack as alone worthy of the name of man, and affects to despise every one else. The Cossack spends the most of his time at the cordons, in expeditions, hunting and fishing. He almost never works at home. His presence in his stanitza is an exception to the rule, but when he is there he lounges. Wine is a common commodity among all the Cossacks, and drunkenness is not so much a universal propensity as it is a rite, the non-fulfilment of which would be regarded as apostasy.

The Cossack looks on a woman as the instrument of his well-being. Only while she is unmarried does he allow her to be idle and make merry; but when she is once a wife he compels her to work for him from youth to the very end of old age. He is thoroughly Oriental in his demand on her obedience and toil. As the result of this state of things, woman, though to all appearances in subjection, becomes powerfully developed both physically and morally, and, as is commonly the case in the East, possesses incomparably more influence and consequence in domestic affairs than in the West. Her seclusion from society and her inurement to hard manual labour give her still more authority and command in domestic affairs. The

Cossack who, in the presence of strangers, regards it as unbecoming to talk affectionately or gossip with his wife, cannot help feeling her superiority when he is left alone with her. His whole house, his whole estate, his whole establishment have been acquired by her, and are maintained solely by her labours and exertions. And though he is obstinately convinced that toil is degrading for a Cossack, and is the proper occupation only of a Nogai labourer or a woman, yet he has a dim consciousness that everything that redounds to his comfort, and that he calls his own, is the result of this toil, and that it is in the power of his mother or his wife, even though he looks on her as his serf, to deprive him of all that makes his life agreeable. – Moreover, the constant hard field labour, and the duties intrusted to them, give a peculiarly independent, masculine character to the "greben" women, and have served to develop in them, to a remarkable degree, physical powers, healthy minds, decision and stability of character. The women are for the most part stronger and more intelligent, better developed and handsomer, than the men. The beauty of the women among the "Grebensky" (or Terek) Cossacks is due to the striking union in them of the purest type of the Tcherkess with the full and powerful build of the northern woman. Their usual dress is Tcherkess: the Tartar shirt, the beshmet, or under-tunic, and the foot-gear called chuvyaki; but they wear the kerchiefs in the Russian way. The wearing of clean, rich and elegant attire, and the decoration of their cottages, belong to the inseparable conditions of their existence."

*

While the monotonous garrison routine of the stanitzi of the Terek still offers the occasional congenial adventure of a foray against their wild mountaineer neighbours, the Astrakhan Cossacks who have their headquarters in the picturesque, but unhealthy metropolis of the lower

Volga, are principally engaged in the lucrative but unwarlike trade of fishing. The Astrakhan Cossacks form a fast disappearing branch of the Cossack race. Originally an offshoot of the Donskoi they are now slowly being absorbed by the neighbouring nonCossack population.

The whole northern end of the shallow sandybottomed Caspian is a vast natural fish-pond. In spite of a yearly catch of countless sturgeon, herring, *beluga, soudak* and other varieties of fish, many of them wholly unknown outside the waters of this finny paradise, the supply seems inexhaustible.

From the Volga fisheries (and those of the Ural) is obtained the world's principal supply of the famous Russian delicacy – caviar; unknown, however, under that name, and always locally called *ikra*. As the Cossack communities of the Volga and Ural have preserved to a great extent ancient exclusive rights to the river fisheries, they are by far the richest of the Cossack armies. These fishcries, which have existed for centuries, are now exploited by the most scientific methods. The never-failing demand for caviar, of both the coarse and finer qualities, always far exceeds the supply. In Russia as well as in Europe, it is a highly expensive delicacy. In the early days of these colonies, salted caviar, packed in little wooden kegs, formed the most acceptable tribute which could be offered to the Russian court, and this delectable product purchased indemnity for many a Cossack misdeed. On account of its portable nature the price of caviar is almost as high in the restaurants of Astrakhan as in the great restaurants of Europe. A true *gourmet* will, however, be rewarded threefold should he make the pious pilgrimage to Astrakhan for the purpose of tasting the silver-grey, nearly unsalted *ikra*, only to be obtained at its best near the place of origin.

*

Just across the administrative boundaries of European Russia lies the little Cossack capital of Uralsk, still in many ways the most characteristic of the Cossack communities. The adventurous history of this frontier stronghold is especially associated with the name of Pougatchev and the great Cossack revolt of the reign of Catherine II. Following the defeat of the armies of the "False Peter III," only accomplished after a long and bitter struggle, the ancient name of *Jaik*, which had formerly distinguished both the Cossacks and their country, was changed to its present name of Uralsk.

On account of their isolation from their neighbours, the *Uralski Kasaki* have preserved many of the manners and customs of the ancient Cossacks, long since abandoned by the Cossacks of the Don. In these rarely visited districts the ancient system of Cossack land tenure and communal existence are still maintained in all their purity. (See Appendix.)

The Cossacks of the Uralsk deserve, perhaps more than any other branch of their race, to be called the true survivors of the old "Free People." For more than three hundred years they have figured in Russian history. To the remnants of ancient tribes, perhaps of Scythian origin, fugitive Russian peasants and other foreigners joined themselves to form the earliest community inhabiting the shores of the *Jaik*. Among these first settlers were many religious refugees, a majority of them belonging to the strange Russian sect known as *Baskolniki* or "Old Believers." These Russian sectarians, rather than obey the reforming edicts of the Tsars who desired to modernize the ritual of the ancient faith, fled to the deserts to worship God after the primitive fashion of their fathers. A census made during the reign of Peter the Great (1723) shows that the colony included the members of several sects of dissenters, many of whom held to creeds stranger than those of the *Baskolniki*. Along the shores of the *Jaik* all who were persecuted and oppressed, whether Poles, Hungarians or Cossacks of the Don, could live their lives as they pleased.

It was not until the end of the eighteenth century that the Russian Government sought to exercise any control other than a nominal supervision over these liberty-loving citizens. It is to be feared, however, that the Cossack Puritans of Uralsk had their own strange ideas of the ethics of freedom: for, as one of their rollicking songs expresses it,

"Formerly we Cossack fellows Sailed at home upon the sea; Our long boats upon the waters Took a toll from Khiv and Persia." As long as these austere brigands confined their attention to the subjects of the Shah and the Khan of Khiva the Russian Government interfered but little with their affairs. It was only when, at the end of the eighteenth century, Russian trade upon the Caspian began to be an important factor that the business of piracy fell upon evil days. However, the great extension which contact with Russian merchants gave to the fishing industry more than made up for the toll which the Cossacks formerly levied on the trade passing near their shores.

An interesting historical note, concerning these "fishing" Cossacks, may be found in Hakluyt's "Voyages." In this account we are told that in 1673, Master Geoffrey Ducket, returning from his fifth voyage for the Muscovy Company, ran afoul of these pirates, when, "by reason of the variety of the winds and dangerous flats of the Caspian Sea" he was riding at anchor near their shores. He tells that "certain Rus Cossacks, which are outlaws or banished men . . . came to us with divers boats under cover of friendship and entered our ship." The suspicious conduct of these visitors, however, soon undeceived the wise British merchants with respect to their intentions and they thereupon took their hatchets and "skowred the hatches."

For many years the Uralski Cossacks have lived as orderly and peaceable an existence as frontier conditions permit. They were among the first to declare their allegiance to the constitutional government after the overthrow of Tsarism in 1917, and have since resisted the tyranny exercised from Moscow and Petrograd by "King Stork" Lenin, with the same courage and determination which they opposed to the officials of "King Log" Nicholas. The leaders of the Soviet movement – realizing the necessity of winning the Cossack element to their doctrines – have tried every method learned from their German teachers, from terrorism to propaganda, to enlist the sympathies of the sturdy *Uralski*. But the excesses of the pandemoniac government at Petrograd have so disgusted the Cossacks that the adherents of the Bolsheviki were none too gently thrown out of their settlements, early in the struggle between order and anarchy.

*

Some 210 miles northwest of Uralsk lies the Cossack capital of Orenburg, a frontier post which has played a famous part in the stirring annals of Russia's conquest of the *khanates* of Central Asia. Several times the entire city has been transferred to another site, but always nearer to the goal of Russia's ambition – the rich oases of Khiva, Merv, Bokhara, and Samarkand, the centre of Mussulman culture and power in the days of the World Empire of Tamerlane.

Between Orenburg and Tashkent a commercially strategic line of railway, which may be said to rank but second in importance to the Trans-Siberian, now unites European Russia with these prosperous Asiatic markets. The wonderful fruits grown in the orchards of Samarkand and

Bokhara were before the present disturbances transported via Orenburg in long trains of refrigerating cars and distributed all over the Moscow area. On the far Chinese frontier a great cotton-raising district had also sprung into existence during the last two decades of imperial government, when the abrogation of the Russo-American commercial treaty caused the government to aim at becoming economically independent in this respect.

The present city of Orenburg, standing on a high bluff, overlooking a boundless sweep of Tartar steppes, is fast losing its Cossack character through the influx of an alien commercial population.

In the neat public gardens of Orenburg, where before the advent of the Bolsheviki a Cossack band discoursed almost nightly to the promenaders, the population of Orenburg could be studied in all the strange variety of its racial elements. Apparently on the best of terms, the Russianized Tartar inhabitants and the military and civil officials of the government here met on common ground. Hither came the comely Tartar maiden (who of her national costume only retained the not unbecoming Tartar headdress) to flirt discreetly with the students of the Cossack military school. On the benches sat Sart and Tartar merchants talking over the day's business with Russian or Armenian shopkeepers.

Ranking after the territory of the Don and Uralsk Cossacks in extent, the land of the Orenburg Cossacks, stretching in a long narrow band along the course of the upper Uralsk River, is far more Cossack in character than the capital city. Yet under the colonial policy of the old imperial government, the fertile land was becoming filled with new-comers of the non-Cossack class – *moujik* colonists from the overcrowded villages of the north, besides Tartar peasants from the south. Even the half-nomad tribesmen, Kirghiz and Kalmoucks, who have wandered over these plains since the days of the Golden Horde, are now beginning to settle in village communities. Often these little agglomerations are composed partly of mud huts or hovels, partly of the old felt tents of the more conservative tribesmen.

Everywhere the virgin soil is capable, even under the most primitive agricultural conditions, of phenomenal returns for labour expended upon it. The statistics of Orenburg show that the population of this province and its dependencies were, before the war, among the most rapidly growing communities of Russia.

The Russian has always been successful as an Asiatic colonist – for reasons worthy of consideration by our new "mandatory" powers. In this "melting-pot" one may study the process, so much freer of "race-pride" than the Anglo-Saxon methods of colonization, which enabled the Tsarist government to fling wide the frontiers of their Empire during the last half of the nineteenth century.

In this task of Europeanization the Cossack has played an important rôle. Fitted by his origin and history to be an intermediary between East and West, he is happily endowed with sympathy and understand for two often irreconcilable viewpoints. Above all, he has none of the fine contempt for the "yellow races" which besets the Anglo-Saxon, not to mention the now happily disarmed apostles of *Kultur*. Aside from the pathetic and ridiculous attempts of the Bolsheviki to introduce their stereotyped Marxian. *kultur* into the world- old Cosmos of Asia – Russia has played a note- worthy rôle in her Asiatic dominions. While showing powers of as imilation, only to be explained by Russian racial history, the rule of Tsarism was generally less resented among her subject nations than England's milder sway in India. Autocracy and its methods came from Asia and is in no sense generally disliked by the vast majority of Asiatics to-day. In its future dealings with these subject people of the old empire a liberalized Russia will find a difficult problem, yet to aid her in this task she will have the organized experience of her Cossack frontiersmen. No one who has had first-hand knowledge of these borderlands can believe for a moment that the Cossack's mission will end until the vast plains of Central Asia have advanced much farther than they have to-day along the paths of Europe's compelling – if not so immeasurably superior – civilization.

Printed in Poland
by Amazon Fulfillment
Poland Sp. z o.o., Wrocław